James Neil

**Kissing**

Its Curious Bible Mentions

James Neil

**Kissing**
*Its Curious Bible Mentions*

ISBN/EAN: 9783337094652

Printed in Europe, USA, Canada, Australia, Japan

Cover: Foto ©Lupo / pixelio.de

More available books at **www.hansebooks.com**

# KISSING:

## ITS CURIOUS BIBLE MENTIONS.

BY

JAMES NEIL, M.A.,

*Formerly Incumbent of Christ Church, Jerusalem, Author of "Palestine Explored" (3rd Thousand), &c. &c.*

LONDON:

SIMPKIN, MARSHALL, & CO.,

4, STATIONERS' HALL COURT.

1885.

# KISSING.

THE East is the very home of warm feelings and demonstrative actions. In the open life of Palestine, to which a hot dry climate and highly primitive manners alike contribute, and which leaves so little place or occasion for privacy, this fact becomes strongly forced upon a stranger's notice. One is especially struck by the frequency and publicity with which the act of kissing occurs. With us such a greeting is confined to near relations and lovers, and is witnessed, for the most part, only in the seclusion of home. In the East it takes place constantly amongst many other persons between whom no such ties exist, and in the presence of all.

This fact alone is a deeply interesting evidence of the genuineness of the Bible. In that sacred book—written in the East, by

A 2

Easterns, and, as to much of it during ages, for Easterns only—although the narrative portions do not amount to more than about one half of the whole, kissing is mentioned no less than fifty times, which is much more often than it would be found in any solemn Western story of the same length.   Again, about half this number of times—as many as twenty-eight—the reference is plainly to men kissing men, a striking confirmation of the Oriental origin of Holy Scripture.  So much for the significance of its frequency in general.  As, however, many of the particular allusions to this practice are but little understood, some are very obscure, and one or two are most important, I purpose in these pages to explain them all, and to point out the exact force and appropriateness of each.

# CHAPTER I.

## KISSING THE HAND, FEET, GROUND, AND GARMENT.

In Palestine and throughout the East, the ordinary mode of showing submission to a superior is by kissing his hand. In my official capacity at Jerusalem I had frequent experience of this when a *fellahh* * (peasant), or a poor *Sephardeem* * (Eastern) Jew came to me to ask a favour, or, on his petition being granted, desired to make a lowly acknowledgment of his gratitude. At such times the poor man would seize the tips of the fingers of my right hand in both of his, and bending down his head (one of the several forms of the "bowing down," or "obeisance," of the Bible) would bring the back of my hand to his lips, impress a kiss, or succession of rapid kisses, upon it, and then raise it so as to touch his forehead. Poor women also under similar circumstances would do the same. Sometimes, though much more rarely, in their eagerness, they kiss the front of the hand as well as the back.

* See Appendix A, on the Fellahhcen and Sephardeem.

This is something more than an ordinary respectful salutation. The latter, called the *teymeeneh*, throughout the East, consists in raising the right hand, with a slight inclination of the head (sometimes instead "bowing down to the earth," and touching the ground with the right hand), and then placing it in succession over the heart, upon the lips, and upon the forehead. But in kissing the hand of another in the way I have just described, there is the distinct act of an inferior admitting, in a warm and demonstrative manner, the authority of a superior, or of a benefactor, or of both in one. I found in my own case that, when any petition was preferred, the attempt to kiss my hand was accompanied by such expressions as "I am thy servant," or "Thou art our father;" chiefly the latter, which sounded strangely indeed when coming with all earnestness from the lips of some white-bearded patriarch, old enough to be my grandfather.

Etiquette, it is true, ordinarily requires that on such occasions the superior make some show of resistance, and politely endeavour to withdraw his hand; while, in some instances, if he desires to appear very gracious, he will return the salutation by pressing his lips on the forehead or cheek of the other. In certain cases, however, this mode of kissing is made compulsory. When a Pasha, an Emeer of the Lebanon, or any other person placed in authority, desires to exact from those beneath him a sign of submission, he will present them his hand and oblige them to kiss it.

Sometimes, though much more rarely when an offended person of rank is approached with a view of obtaining his pardon, the suppliant will "kiss his feet," which is usually done by touching the feet of the superior with his right hand, and then kissing the hand with which he has so touched, and placing it on his forehead. When we read that the woman in the house of Simon the Pharisee "kissed" the feet of Christ at the time of anointing them, it is possible that the action was performed in this way.* The feet are, however, sometimes actually kissed with the lips in this lowliest form of greeting.

Nearly allied with the last is the abject act of kissing the ground, or dust, upon which

* Luke vii. 37, 38, 45.

a superior has trodden. It is apparently to this extravagant, but still to be witnessed, way of doing homage, that the Psalmist refers, when speaking of the entire submission of the hitherto unconquered *Bedaween* Arabs during Messiah's millennial reign—

> "The dwellers in the desert shall bow *before Him*,
> And *His enemies* shall lick *the dust*" *—

a strong way of saying, "they shall press their lips on the dusty ground which His steps have trodden."

In another description of that glorious time, setting forth the menial offices that Gentile kings and queens will delight to do for the sons, and even for the despised *daughters*, of the House of Israel, the passage concludes with a picture of the prostrate homage of these royal personages, who will kiss the very ground over which a Jew has passed—

> "They shall bow down to thee *with* [*their*] *faces* [*toward the*] *earth*,
> And shall lick up *the dust of thy feet*." †

---

\* Psalm lxxii. 9. The reader is requested to observe that the words in this and all the following quotations from Holy Scripture which are printed in italics are words which the Holy Spirit has rendered emphatic. For an explanation of this he is referred to Appendix B, on Emphasis in Biblical Hebrew and Greek.

† Isaiah xlix. 23.

The ground, like the feet, is often kissed by a man's stooping down to touch it with his right hand, and then kissing the hand with which he has so touched and placing it upon his forehead.

There is yet another similar mode of showing servile submission—namely, by taking hold of and kissing the end of the Eastern loose flowing cloak, either the square, sleeveless, brown and white striped, goat's or camel's hair sackcloth *abayeh* of the *Bedaween* and *Fellahheen*, or the rich coloured cloth *jibbeh*, or *beneesh*, which takes its place amongst the *Belladeen*, or townspeople. This salutation necessitates the stooping down in a deep obeisance at the same time. When Saul, in his agony of despair, was entreating Samuel to help him once more to seek Jehovah, as the latter "turned about to go away," Saul "laid strong hold upon the wing of his outer robe"—that is, its "loose flowing end"—in a humble and supplicating manner, most probably intending to kiss it.* At the time of the Millennium we are told that "ten men out of all languages of the foreign nations shall lay strong hold, yea, they shall lay

* I Samuel xv. 27.

strong hold, of the wing of a Jew "—that is,
"the loose flowing end of his outer robe "—or,
in other words, invoke his aid and show him
the lowliest submission by stooping down to
seize the corner of his cloak to kiss it.*

Some other scriptural allusions to this
kind of salutation, more especially that ordinary form of it which consists in kissing
the hand, have, I think, been overlooked.
When Jethro came to meet Moses encamped
with all Israel at the foot of Sinai, bringing
with him his daughter and her children,
"Moses went out to meet his father-in-law,
and bowed down and kissed him "—that is, he
showed him great reverence in the sight of all
the people, bowing down, seizing his hand,
kissing it, and pressing it to his forehead.†

Samuel, we are told, "took a vessel of oil,
and poured it upon his (Saul's) head, and
kissed him, and said, 'Is it not because
Jehovah has anointed thee to be chief *over
His inheritance?*'"‡   In this way he first
anointed him as a ruler, then immediately
proceeded to pay him homage by kissing his

---

* Zechariah viii. 23.   Akin to this was the action of the
woman with an issue of blood, and of the sick in the land
of Gennesaret (Matthew ix. 20 ; xiv. 36).

Exodus xviii. 7.                    ‡ I Samuel x. I.

hand, and finally explained these acts to signify his appointment by God as the King of Israel.

A bold and beautiful figure drawn from this custom occurs in that Messianic hymn, the second Psalm, where the kings and judges of the earth are called upon to serve "Jehovah's Anointed," the Son of God—

> "Eagerly kiss the Son, lest He be angry,
> And you perish [from, or as to, the] Way." *

This must allude to kissing the hand, or possibly the feet or garment, for the only other kiss given by one man to another— namely, that upon the cheek or the forehead—is never offered to one of a superior rank, much less to a king. Our Blessed Lord claims the believer's entire surrender, humble supplication, and grateful love; and it will be seen, from what has been said above, that all of these—submission, dependence, and gratitude—are skilfully included in the command to pay homage to the Son by kissing His hand!

It is most interesting, and for Jews and objectors most important, to observe that

---

Psalm ii. 12. The Hebrew word "kiss," here, נַשְּׁקוּ *nash-shĕ-koo*, being in the piel, or intensive, structure of the verb is, as I have rendered it, "eagerly, or diligently, kiss."

faith in Jesus came, at its commencement, to be commonly called "the Way," alike by Jews, Gentiles, and the Church of God. In the Revised Version, the word "Way," in six passages of the Acts, is very rightly printed with a capital W, as a proper name given to the way of salvation preached by the Apostles.* To the believer this name is the more suggestive and appropriate, seeing that Jesus has declared Himself to be "The Way, the truth, and the life ;" or, as this well-known Hebrew idiom should be rendered, "The *true* and *living* Way," and has added "*no one* cometh unto the Father but by me."† This very name, therefore, "the Way," given to the Gospel, reminds His people that the Lord Christ, as a Personal Saviour, is the Alpha and Omega (the A and Z) of the New Covenant, the Object, Author, and Finisher of saving faith.‡

It is usual amongst commentators to repre-

---

* Acts ix. 2 ; xix. 9; xix. 23 ; xxii. 4; xxiv. 14; xxiv. 22. See Revised Version. Also notice Acts xvi. 17, and xviii. 25, 26, in which last verse "the Way of God" may be a Hebrew form for "the *great* Way," just as "a trembling of God" is "a *great* trembling" (1 Samuel xiv. 15), "cedars of God" are "*great* cedars" (Psalm lxxx. 10), and "mountains of God" are "*great* mountains" (Psalm xxxvi. 6), &c.

† John xiv. 6.          ‡ Hebrews xii. 2.

sent the traitor Judas as delivering up Christ by kissing His cheek ; and they have dwelt upon the deep heinousness of an act of familiarity upon which no other man is said to have ventured. But was this really the case? There seems to me no reason to conclude that Iscariot took any such liberty with the person of the Lord Christ. His approach was, to all appearance, a very humble one. He addressed the Saviour as " Rabbi," or rather, as we read in the account in Mark's more graphic Gospel, " Rabbi, Rabbi," which is literally, " My great one, My great one," a term of considerable respect had it been used only once, but here much intensified, according to the Hebrew and Arabic idiom, by the figure of Repetition.*

It is also important to notice that two Evangelists tell us that "Judas kissed Him much or eagerly " (κατεφίλησεν, *katephilēsen*),† a strong expression which has been a great difficulty to the commentators, for they could not suppose that the traitor went out of his way to

---

* Mark xiv. 45. Some authorities, it is true, omit the second "Rabbi" in this verse, but it is retained by Alford and many others. It would seem that Judas generally addressed our Lord as "Rabbi." (See Matthew xxvi. 25.)

† Matthew xxvi. 49 ; Mark xiv. 45.

kiss our Lord very eagerly, by way of affectionate greeting, at a moment so awful. The very thought of such a thing is monstrous. But to kiss the hand in this eager, ostentatious way as a sign of lowly submission, for instance, to give several kisses instead of one, and on the front of the hand as well as the back (which I have already shown is sometimes the case), is much more natural, and quite in keeping with the trembling and awe that may well have seized his soul.

Just as in the words, " kiss the Son," we have an allusion to kissing His hand and not His face, so, when we read that Judas "eagerly kissed" Christ, it is in all probability meant that he paid Him publicly the homage of a disciple by seizing and ostentatiously, or repeatedly, kissing His hand. While this explanation in no way lessens the traitor's guilt, it makes the scene, from an Eastern standpoint, far more life-like.

I have said that a superior usually condescends to snatch away his hand in order to prevent its ˙being kissed. In this case, the inferior, if much in earnest, immediately kisses his own fingers, and then puts them against his forehead, as much as to say he would have done the same to the other if he could. This seems evidently the idea that underlies that act of worship with which Mohammedans have been observed to begin their prayers—namely, bringing their two thumbs together, kissing them three times, and touching their foreheads with them. They cannot kiss the hand of the unseen God and raise it to their brow, in token of lowly submission, earnest supplication, or grateful acknowledgment, and so they kiss their own hands instead.*

Here, doubtless, we have the full force of Jehovah's allusion, " I have left seven thousand in Israel, all the knees which have not bowed to Baal, and every mouth which has not kissed him." † In the same sense we must understand the expression employed by the prophet Hosea to describe the apostate worship at Bethel and Dan, "they eagerly [or repeatedly] kiss *calves*."‡ There is an interesting passage in the *Octavius* of Minutius Felix, which is an apology for the Faith of Christ, written between 166 and 198 A.D.

---

* Possibly their kissing the back of both hands joined together is significant of an intensive form of submissive acknowledgment.

† 1 Kings xix. 18.    ‡ Hosea xiii. 2.

It is in the form of a dialogue, which takes its rise from an incident told in the following words: ."Cæcilius (a heathen going towards the sea along the banks of the Tiber at Rome), observing an image of Serapis, raised his hand to his mouth, as is the custom of the superstitious common people, and pressed a kiss on it with his lips."* The words in which Job declares his innocence of the crime of idolatry become very clear and striking when viewed in this light—

"If I beheld Light [i.e., the Sun] when it shined,
And moon gloriously proceeding on,
And my heart was secretly enticed,
And my mouth kissed *my hand*,
*This* also were a crime to be judged,
For I should have denied God above." †

* *Octavius*, chap. ii.　　　　† Job xxxi. 26, 27.

# CHAPTER II.

## KISSING THE DOCUMENT.

IT is usual throughout the East to show respect to any written document containing the commands of a person high in authority by raising it to the forehead, and kissing it either before or after so doing. The Sultan's *firman*, or, amongst the *Bedaween*, the letter of any important Sheikh, would be thus received in token of submission to their power.

It is to this practice apparently that reference is made by Egypt's despotic Pharaoh, when, investing Joseph with supreme authority as the Grand Vizier, or Prime Minister, he said, " *Upon thy mouth* shall all my people kiss." * The word " mouth " occurs in Scripture, for " commandment."† The full meaning of Pharaoh's declaration is, " *upon thy commandment* (that is, when formally written down) shall all my people kiss." It was immediately followed by the significant and explanatory act of delivering

* Genesis xli. 40.    † Genesis xlv. 21, &c.

B

up to the new minister "the Great Seal" of the kingdom. We read in the next verse but one, "and Pharaoh took off his ring from his hand and put it upon Joseph's hand"—that is, he invested him with the royal signet-ring, "the Great Seal" of Egypt, by which the royal assent was given to all state documents.*

This use of the monarch's ring, giving it such immense value, is implied to have been in existence eleven hundred years later in the land of Judah ; for Jeremiah, in the name of Jehovah, cries—

" Though Coniah, the son of Jehoiakim, the king of Judah,
Were a signet-ring upon [my] right hand,
Yet *from there* would I pluck thee !" †

After another hundred years we find just the same custom in Persia. Ahasuerus "the king took his signet from his hand and gave it to Haman," and the latter then wrote out the decree of destruction, " and sealed it with the king's signet." ‡

Possessed of Pharaoh's signet-ring, Joseph, from his official position, could, as easily as Haman, get "the king's secretaries" to write down from his mouth any edict he might

---

* Genesis xli. 42.  † Jeremiah xxii. 24.
‡ Esther iii. 10, 12.  See also viii. 2, 8, 10.

think fit to dictate. He could then, after the present primitive and uniform fashion, rub a little ink, with his finger, on the engraved face of Pharaoh's ring, and press it at the foot of the papyrus roll so written, the contents of which would, by the resulting impression, be converted into an absolute decree. It would only be necessary to present such a document to any of the Egyptian Pashas of that day, and he would reverently raise it to his lips and kiss it in token of submission, just as his modern representative does to-day.

A similar explanation, I have no doubt, is required by a still more difficult allusion, and one which has been the occasion of great perplexity to the commentators—namely, the words of the wise man, which are in our version—

"[Every man] shall kiss [his] lips
That giveth a right answer." *

Spoken as they are of one high in authority who gives just decisions, the words standing thus are worse than meaningless from an Eastern standpoint. Even men who are friends and equals only kiss one another on the cheek. It would be insult instead of

* Proverbs xxiv. 26.

B 2

respect, rebellion rather than homage, for suitors to dare to kiss even the cheek—but how much more the lips!—of an Oriental judge.

But a right translation of the verse gives a meaning that is perfectly appropriate, in complete harmony with the context, and full of force. This true rendering, the very opposite of that in our Bible, is as follows—

"[ *The*] *two lips* [*each of them*] shall kiss
  That which returns [an answer of] straightforward
  words." *

It should be observed that the whole passage from which the verse I am explaining is taken contains a description of the results of partial and impartial judgment. The East is

---

* Proverbs xxiv. 26. This is the general sense of the rendering in the Septuagint, the ancient Authorised Version of the Old Testament in use in our Saviour's time, and from which most of the quotations of Scripture in the New Testament appear to have been made—"χείλη δὲ φιλήσουσιν ἀποκρινόμενα λόγους ἀγαθούς" (*cheilē de philēsousin apokrinomena logous agathous*). The participle שׁיב, *maisheev*, from *shoov*, "to return," which commences the second member of the verse, may mean either "he that causes to return [an answer]," or "the thing which causes to return," &c.; but the Septuagint just quoted renders it like the latter—that is, as referring to a document and not a person. See Appendix C., on the Logical Concord, for the full proof of the rendering I have adopted.

still cursed, as it appears to have been in
Bible times, with corrupt and unjust judges,
who take "*a gift out of the bosom* "—that is, "a
bribe from a man's breast pocket "—a secret
bribe—" to pervert the ways of judgment." *
Owing to this, it is well known in most
parts of Palestine that it is utterly useless to
bring an action, or appear as a plaintiff in any
cause, unless you are prepared to bribe the
judge. Hence the force and appropriateness
of the frequent references to a similar state of
things in the Word of God. Where the judges
are corrupt, the poor, the people at large, can
no longer hope for any kind of justice. In
this sad sense, truly

"The rich man's wealth is his *strong* city,
The *destruction of the poor* is their poverty !" †

Our Blessed Lord often appears to allude
to such a state of society when denouncing
the robbery and wrong committed by the
wealthy scribes and Pharisees by means of
legal frauds.‡ It is in this light that we must
read all our Saviour's warnings to the rich, and

* Proverbs xvii. 23. † Proverbs x. 15.
‡ Matthew xxiii. 14; Mark xii. 40; Luke xx. 47. The
best authorities, however, omit Matt. xxiii. 14 from the
text (see Revised Version).

His words of comfort to the poor.*    His parable of the unjust judge was a terribly familiar
illustration to all His hearers.    In the General
Epistle of James there is a graphic reference
to these judicial frauds, as forming a constant
feature of Eastern life.    " Do not *the wealthy*
oppress you, and *themselves* drag you into the
courts of justice ? "    " Come now, you wealthy,
weep and yell † for your miseries that are coming upon [you].    *Your wealth* has putrefied,‡
and *your garments* have become *moth-eaten ;
your gold and silver* have become rusted, and
*the rust of them* will be *a witness against you,* and
will eat your fleshy parts like fire.    You have
laid up treasure in [the] *last* days.    Behold, *the
hire of the labourers who cut down your fields,
which has been kept back by reason of you,* cries
out ;  and *the cries of the reapers* have entered
*into the ears of the Lord of Sabaoth* . . . you

* Addressed to the rich: Matthew vi. 24 ; xix. 23, 24 ;
Mark x. 23; Luke viii. 14 ; xii. 16–21 ; xvi. 1–11 ; xvi. 19–23.
Addressed to the poor : Matthew xi. 5 ; Luke vi. 20 ; xiv.
13 ; xxi. 3, &c.

† For the interesting meaning of this word "yell," see
Appendix D, on the Tahleel, Olooleh, or Woolwal.

‡ The "riches" here by being said to be "putrefied" are
shown to be such as corn, wine, oil, and other agricultural
produce (the usual wealth of Palestine), which they had
amassed like the Rich Fool (Luke xii. 18), but which had
been acquired in their case by fraud.

have condemned, you have killed the just [man] ; he does not resist you."*

Now let the whole passage in the Book of Proverbs be read in this light :—

"Respect of persons in judgment is not good.
He that says to the violently-wicked, '*Righteous* art thou,'
The nations shall curse him ;
As to tribes they shall abhor him.
But *to those that convict* [*him*] it shall be pleasant ;
And *upon them* shall come a *good* blessing.
[*The*] *two lips* [*each of them*] shall kiss
That which returns [an answer of] straightforward words."†

That is to say, "those who justify the wicked shall be cursed by the people, but those who fearlessly 'convict' (יָכַח, *yakhahh*, 'to convict,' or 'punish') such violent evil-doers shall have 'a *good* blessing' invoked upon them. The decrees of such a just judge shall be seized and fervently kissed by all to whom they come, in token of men's submission to his righteous decisions." And, as an Eastern king exercises also the office of Lord Chief Justice, the words apply equally to the reception of all royal edicts and *firmans* of an upright and beneficent character.

In their fullest sense, they set before us the righteousness of the Lord Christ, " the *Great*

* James ii. 6 ; v. 1-6. † Proverbs xxiv. 23-26.

King," the supreme "Judge," to whom the
Father has "committed *all judgment*."* He,
indeed, both with regard to this life and that
which is to come, has "*judged righteous* judgment," as recorded in Holy Scripture, and all
who know and love the truth delight, as it were
to kiss that Blessed Book, in acceptance of its
Divine decrees, and in humble acknowledgment of their justice and mercy.

It is very interesting to observe that the
practice of kissing the Gospels, when taking
an oath in a court of justice, would seem to
have its origin in this ancient act of saluting a
document in token of reverence for the authority of him who sent it. Bending down,
when sworn, to kiss the Scriptures, is, therefore, no mere superstitious usage; but, on the
contrary, a confession, formerly well understood, of the existence and power of God,
and of submission to the commands of His
written Word.

* Matthew v. 35; John v. 22, 27; Revelation xix. 16.

# CHAPTER III.

## KISSING THE FACE.

WE now come to a very grave difficulty connected with the Bible references to kissing. I allude to the Apostolic injunction to believers to salute one another in this way; a command which, I imagine, has been almost universally misunderstood. We first find it in the Epistle to the Romans, " Salute one another with a holy kiss."* Three times afterwards, the Apostle Paul, writing under inspiration, solemnly repeats the same command,† slightly varying it once in writing a second time to the Church at Corinth, when, by inverting the order of the noun and adjective, he gives the well-known Greek emphasis, " a *holy* kiss."‡ Possibly the stress on the word "*holy*" here is a gentle rebuke to the strife and party spirit by which the Corinthian Church was rent. § Once again it

---

* Romans xvi. 16.

† 1 Corinthians xvi. 20; 2 Corinthians xiii. 12; 1 Thessalonians v. 26.

‡ 2 Corinthians xiii. 12.

§ 1 Corinthians i. 12-14; iii. 3, 4.

occurs, and this time in the first letter of the
Apostle of the Circumcision ; Peter agreeing
with Paul in enforcing the same truth.
Although the title of the kiss is different, the
injunction to bestow it is just the same,
" Salute one another with a *loving* kiss." *

Now two quite opposite errors have beset
this subject, the one, which has been prevalent
in the Church at large for very many centuries,
making the Apostles to mean *nothing*, and
the other making them to mean *too much*.
The latter is now reviving amongst some
bodies of earnest believers. These, while
commendably anxious to yield a loyal obe-
dience to the letter of Scripture, have, not
unnaturally, mistaken the *sense* of that letter,
and are introducing, in connection with worship, a custom of kissing amongst their male
and female members.

It is certainly impossible to doubt that the
command to kiss, thus solemnly repeated five
times, is, in its true meaning, binding upon
the followers of Christ. I will now try to
show the nature of this true meaning, which,
had it been known, would have led to the
observance of the injunction, and thus have

* I Peter v. 14.

saved us from much of the present worldliness of the Churches.

First, let me prove that this command *must* have been addressed *to men with respect to men only, and to women with respect to women only.* At the time when all the Epistles were written, worship would, doubtless, be conducted in accordance with the strict customs of the East, the men being separated from the women. The men would meet in one part of the building, or room, and the women in another. The men would salute each other, and the women might do the same; but, throughout the East, it is altogether contrary to what has ever been considered "chaste" or "of good fame" for a man and a woman to greet one another in public, even though members of the same family. Indeed, it is not allowed by the strictness of Oriental etiquette to address a word to a woman whom one does not know. Hence, in part, the embarrassment of our Lord's disciples when they found Him in conversation with the stranger at Jacob's well; for we read, "they marvelled that he was talking *with a woman!*"*

---

* John iv. 27. Observe, not "*the* woman," as in the Authorised Version, but "*a* woman." See Revised Version.

What applies to meetings in the synagogues, and in the rooms afterwards set apart for the worship of the Church, applies equally to all social gatherings. On such occasions, when guests assemble, the men are met and entertained by the host in one apartment, and the women by his wife, mother, or daughters in another, and these two companies are carefully kept apart, and never exchange greetings.

This is universal. The idea of men and women of different families, in the lands where the Epistles were written, and at the time of the beginning of the Gospel, meeting freely together in the way that we should do now, either in their homes, or at their religious assemblies, is one of those grave misconceptions which could occur only to a Western mind. It is most probable that, when, as disciples of Christ, women were first fully placed in spiritual privileges on a level with men, and were allowed to attend the meetings of the Church, it was still necessary, in that transition period, for them to be veiled as well as to keep to their own part of the room.

Such appears to be the natural meaning of the passage where the Apostle Paul says, "*Every woman praying or prophesying with* *her head unveiled* dishonours her head," and decides "let her be veiled."* Indeed, it would seem that it was partly because any such act would require her unveiling, that the Apostle forbids a woman to speak in the public assemblies, saying, " Let *the women* (or *wives*) keep silence *in the Churches.*"† In the very next verse he cries, " It is *a shame* for a woman to speak in the Church," and this word " shame " ( αἰσχρὸν, *aischron*) is the very word he uses when he says, " *If it is a shame for a woman to be shorn or shaven*, let her be veiled." ‡

The difficult words that occur in the tenth verse, " the woman ought to have [a sign of] *authority* on her head, because of the angels," have been held to point in the same direction. They seem to be a figurative way of saying " she ought to have a veil on her head as the sign of her husband's authority over her," because of " the messengers," or "angels," the ministers, who would, at that time, have been sadly disconcerted had they been called upon

---

* 1 Corinthians xi. 5, 6. See Revised Version. The word "*unveiled*" in this verse has an emphasis of its own above the rest.

† 1 Corinthians xiv. 34.   ‡ 1 Corinthians xi. 6.

to preach to an assembly of unveiled women, which Dr. Thomson, in a very interesting passage, shows would be equally the case in Syria to-day.* It is important to observe that these words are addressed not to a Church in Asia, nor to Hebrews only, but to the Church at Corinth, a Gentile Church in a Greek city. From this we learn that, in the age of the Apostles, the Eastern customs with regard to the sexes at public worship prevailed also in the Western world.

It is out of the question, therefore, to suppose that the command to kiss has reference to other than the respective greetings of men with men, and of women with women. Every idea connected with the stringent proprieties of a land like Palestine, owing to the seclusion of females and the separation of the sexes, requires this limitation, which there was no need whatever to specify in a Revelation addressed to Easterns, or to those accustomed to Eastern usages, and published about the midst of the first century. Had anything been intended so strange, nay, so monstrous to their notions, as the fact of all men indiscriminately kissing all women, and that,

* *The Land and the Book*, p. 31.

too, in a Church like the Corinthian, where such terrible impurity had crept in,* it must have been specially and distinctly stated, and that with restrictions to guard against its abuse.

Moreover, had it been otherwise, such indiscriminate salutation between men and women, commanded to take place at their secret meetings, would have formed a very damaging charge sure to have been brought against the Church by the early Pagan and Jewish objectors. Anything so eminently contrary to "the things" that were "chaste (ἁγνὰ, hagna)" and "of good fame"† in the world of that day, resting, too, as it would have done, upon documentary evidence, must have been very specially and constantly singled out, and held up to scathing reprobation or scandalous reproach. It is well known that reckless and shameful charges were brought by unbelieving Jews and heathen against the Churches of Christ because of their secluded assemblies, especially those for the administration of the Lord's Supper. But I can nowhere find that the command to kiss was made the ground of any such charge; and this is, in itself, a proof that it was not

* 1 Corinthians v. † Philippians iv. 8.

taken to apply to a salutation between men
and women.*

I have dealt, so far, with the words themselves, but I will now submit indisputable
evidence that the interpretation given above
is identical with the interpretation put upon
the passage by the primitive Church. It is
well known that this kiss was practised
amongst the followers of Christ for a long
time. It was called "the kiss of greeting,"
and also " the kiss of peace ; " indeed we find
it sometimes called simply "the peace," and
this name implies that it was a kiss of ordinary
friendly greeting. " Peace be to you " was
from earliest times, and is to this hour, the
usual spoken salutation throughout the East
—the friendly " how do you do ? " of English;
the proper reply to it being "*upon you* be
peace." † One special time when they were
in the habit of thus greeting, Justin Martyr
tells us, in his *Apology*, was during Divine

* I say this after having diligently searched the following
answers to heathen objectors of the first three centuries :
Justin Martyr's *First and Second Apologies*, Tatian's *Dis-
course to the Greeks*, Athenagoras' *Plea for the Christians*,
Minutius Felix' *Octavius*, Tertullian's *Ad Nationes*, and his
*Apology*, and Origen's *Against Celsus*.

† Genesis xxix. 6; xliii. 23 ; Exodus xviii. 7 ; Judges
xix. 20 ; 1 Samuel xxv. 6, &c. &c.

Service, just before partaking of the Holy
Communion. His words are, "Prayers being
ended, we salute one another with a kiss.
There is then brought to that one of the
brethren who was presiding bread and a cup
of wine."* This way of putting it, albeit
precisely the same as the language of its
institution, leaves it uncertain *by* and *to whom*
such salutation was given.

But in the *Apostolical Constitutions*, a
work dating in part probably from the third
century, where a fuller description of Worship
is found, the matter is finally cleared up.
The author says, "On the other side let the
laics (the 'people,' or rather 'men') sit·with
all silence and good order ; and the women,
let them sit also *separately*, keeping silence."
After a lengthy account of the service following upon this, he adds, "Then let the men
salute one another, and the women one
another, with the kiss in the Lord."† Here,

* *The First Apology of Justin Martyr*, chapter lxv.

† *Apostolical Constitutions*, Book ii., chap. 57. This work
probably assumed its present form in the fifth or sixth century,
but Canon Westcott speaks of that part of it which describes
worship in the second Book as "in all likelihood as old as the
third century." There is a somewhat similar statement in Book
viii., chap. 11, of the *Apostolical Constitutions*, which is considered to be a much later addition to the first seven books.

C

not only are the women to sit separately, as was universally the case in the early Church, but they are only "to kiss *one another*," while the men are limited to kissing men. This is made particularly plain in the Greek original, as, unlike English, the word "one another" is used in a masculine form where the men are spoken of, and in a feminine form in the case of the women. The passage is, "Let the men salute *one another-of-the-masculine-gender*, and the women *one another-of-the-feminine-gender*, with a kiss," &c. *

This plain statement decides the point in question beyond the possibility of doubt, and the fact that, at a later period, "the kiss of peace," or "the *loving* kiss," gave rise to scandal, and was therefore discountenanced, and fell into final disuse, only shows that it had come to be as much misunderstood amongst the Church of that day as it is generally amongst us.

The reader will observe that the above

---

* εἶτα καὶ ἀσπαζέσθωσαν ἀλλήλους οἱ ἄνδρες καὶ ἀλλήλας αἱ γυναῖκες τὸ ἐν κυρίῳ φίλημα, *eita kai aspazesthōsan allēlous hoi andres, kai allēlas hai gunaikes, to en kuriō philēma.* The reader is here referred to Appendix E, on the Kiss of Peace, for the correction of a grave error on this subject in Smith's *Dictionary of Christian Antiquities.*

explanation entirely removes the principal difficulty that has hitherto been felt in the texts which tell us to " salute one another with a holy kiss "—namely, that such embrace was to be given indifferently to either sex. That it should have been lost sight of is not surprising, on two grounds. First, because the spread of the Gospel, by raising woman and bringing into the world a new purity, abolished in Western Lands the state of things existing before. Secondly, because the words " salute one another with a holy kiss " are figurative. They present the figure of Ellipsis or Omission. The words in this case omitted, but understood, being " men and women respectively."

This figure of Ellipsis is common to all languages, but peculiar to the concise tongues of the East, and pre-eminent in Biblical Hebrew and Greek. It is a fact, albeit one that is unhappily but little understood, that the Holy Scriptures abound with figurative language generally in a very high degree, probably beyond any other work; for it may be truly said that almost every error that has crept into the Church has been founded on taking a figurative expression in a literal sense! The whole subject of figurative language, notwithstanding its immense importance to the Biblical student, has hitherto altogether failed to receive sufficient attention. One of the ablest works, and, as far as I am aware, the only exhaustive popular one in English dealing with the study of figures of speech, scarcely sold in this country in the ordinary way to the extent of twenty copies ! *

Now that we see what the words do not and cannot mean, the way is prepared for perceiving their true import. There are two distinct kinds of kissing in connection with the customs of Eastern salutation. One is that which I have already described, of inferiors in their character of dependents or suppliants—namely, the kissing of a superior's hand, varied sometimes by kissing his feet, the hem of his garment, or the dust on which he has trodden. The other is that which takes place in an exchange of greeting between two equals.

When these latter are relatives or old and dear friends, they embrace one another, espe-

* *The Might and Mirth of Literature. A Treatise on Figurative Language.* By John Walker Vilant Macbeth. Messrs. Sampson Low & Co. 1876.

cially after a long absence, in the following
manner. Each, in turn, places his head, face
downwards, upon the other's left shoulder,
and afterwards kisses him upon the right
cheek, and then reverses the action, by
placing his head similarly upon the other's
right shoulder and kissing him upon the left
cheek. This exceedingly impressive and picturesque mode of embrace was the way in
which Esau greeted Jacob, for we are told
"he fell on his neck and kissed him;" in
which Joseph and Benjamin acknowledged
their blood relationship, and in which Joseph
welcomed and reassured the whole of his
troubled brethren. Such, also, was the
warm and tender greeting given by the father
in the parable to the Prodigal Son, as unex-
pected as Esau's similar reception of his
trembling brother ; and the affectionate part-
ing salutation between Paul and the elders of
the Ephesian Church.* Between the first

* Genesis xxxiii. 4 ; xlv. 14, 15 ; Luke xv. 20 ; Acts xx.
37. It should be noted that in these last two instances
the word is καταφιλέω, *kataphileō*, "to kiss much or
eagerly," that is, repeatedly, and with much warm expression
of feeling. A precisely similar force is also given in the
Hebrew of Genesis xlv. 15, which is, "Moreover he (Joseph
when making himself known) eagerly kissed all his brethren"
—the verb "kiss" being in the *piel* structure, which gives

and last mentions of this custom stretches a
period of more than 1800 years! What
wonder then that, after the lapse of another
1800 years, we find it still the same in the
changeless life of Bible Lands!

When a kindly, but somewhat more formal
and respectful, salutation passes between those
of the same rank, they will take hold of each
other's beards and kiss them. Women also
greet their husbands, and children their
fathers, in like manner. It is a great insult
to take hold of a man's beard on any occasion but that of kissing it. Treacherous Joab
took advantage of this special form of embrace
to assassinate the brother commander of whom
he was jealous. Saluting him with the words
"'Art thou *well*, my brother?' . . . Joab
took hold of Amasa's beard [with the] right
hand, to kiss him," that is, "to kiss his beard,"
and, when the other was thus thrown off his
guard, stabbed him by a left-handed thrust
with a short sword.*

There is, however, another common occasion of kissing amongst men. The saluta-

the sense of doing a thing diligently, or forcibly. A beautiful touch is thus imparted to the picture of his magnanimous
treatment of those poor, trembling, guilty brethren.
  * 2 Samuel xx. 9, 10.

tion which passes in polite society between a host and those of his guests who are in a similar station of life, consists in placing the right hand upon the other's left shoulder and kissing his right cheek, and then laying the left hand on his right shoulder and kissing his left cheek. It was in this way that Absalom saluted the people who came to kiss his hand, for, "it was so that when a man came nigh to do him obeisance he put forth his hand, and took hold of him, and kissed him," that is, he flattered the common people, whom he sought to draw into his conspiracy, by treating them as friends and equals.*

Simon the Pharisee, with whom our Lord went "to eat"—either to breakfast at midday or to dine at sunset—in addition to the other ordinary customs of reception at the houses of the wealthy—namely, having his guests' feet washed by one servant, and their persons sprinkled with perfume by another, greeted them each, in this usual way, with a kiss on the cheek. But it would seem that he did not care to appear too intimate with the lowly "Man of Sorrows," the despised carpenter-prophet, and Our Blessed Lord gently up-

* 2 Samuel xv. 5.

braids him for his unkind and discourteous
conduct in the words "thou gavest *me* no
*kiss*." * This was the neglectful reception ac-
corded by the proud, cold-hearted, uncon-
verted Pharisee, a gross breach of the laws of
Eastern hospitality, towards one whom he had
specially invited to a feast ; and in striking
contrast was that of the humble, loving, saved
outcast, who was in no way responsible for
the honours of the house, but of whom the
Master tells us, "*she, since the time I came in,*
has not ceased to eagerly kiss *my* feet " † —
the lowliest of all modes of grateful homage !
No excuse can be alleged for Simon on the
ground of his regarding Jesus as a prophet,
or as a great rabbi, and therefore feeling too
much respect to treat Him as an equal, for,
in that case, he ought to have reverently
saluted Him as a superior, by kissing His
hand, to say nothing of being doubly careful
to see that His feet were washed and His
head anointed.

There is another more formal mode of salu-

* Luke vii. 45. As our Lord further points out, Simon's
neglect was so marked as even to leave His feet unwashed,
and His head unsprinkled with oil.

† Luke vii. 45. The word here is καταφιλοῦσά, *kataphil-
ousa*, "kissing much or eagerly."

tation between those of a similar station of
life when meeting in the ordinary way. In
this case they join their right hands, simply
placing them one to the other, and then each
kisses his own hand and puts it to his lips and
forehead, sometimes to his forehead only, or
over his heart, and at others over his heart,
merely, without kissing it.*

It was by laying either the hand or the
head on the shoulder, and kissing the cheek,
that Laban greeted his nephew Jacob ; Aaron,
his brother Moses; David, his friend Jonathan,
his son Absalom, and his aged benefactor
Barzillai.†

There is a beautiful allegorical allusion to

---

* Akin to this is the practice amongst the *fellahheen* of
seizing each other's hands, often for a minute together, not
shaking them as with us, but clasping them, so as each to
place his fingers in turn over the other's thumb, repeating
alternately "*selamat,*" " Peace," or, " How do you do ? " and
" *teiyibeen,*" " Are you well ? " Sometimes this is done by
clapping each other's hands very smartly twenty or thirty
times instead of clasping them, while they repeat these
words—a very hearty mode of salutation, confined to the
*fellahheen* class.

† Genesis xxix. 13 ; Exodus iv. 27 ; 1 Samuel xx. 41 ;
2 Samuel xiv. 33. In Genesis xxix. 13, the word "kissed "
is in the *piel* structure, meaning "eagerly kissed." On two
other occasions referring to Laban, Genesis xxxi. 28, and
Genesis xxxi. 55, the word is also in the *piel* structure, for
Jacob's uncle appears to have been as demonstrative as he
was deceitful.

this kind of salutation, that well brings out its use as a figure of speech. The Psalmist, setting forth God's promised salvation, tells how the work of grace, through Christ's atonement, reconciles the Divine Righteousness to Peace, from which in a world of sin it had hitherto been estranged.

> " *Mercy* and *Truth* are met together,
> *Righteousness* and *Peace* have kissed," *

or, as we should say, " have shaken hands," that is, have met as friends and equals on good terms with one another !

Now one of these three latter greetings— namely, falling on the neck and kissing, kissing the beard, or laying the hand on the shoulder and kissing the cheek—most probably the last—must be the salutation intended in the apostolic injunction, "salute one another with a holy kiss." Viewed in this light, the command becomes not only natural and reasonable in itself, but pregnant with important meaning. It was intended to teach the Church of God that, as believers, all its members were to meet on a friendly and equal footing, and in a way that was to remind them of their common brotherhood in Christ. All

* Psalm lxxxv. 10.

distinctions of caste and rank among the people of the Lord, when gathered together in the character of His people, should, therefore, be completely laid aside.

Kissing the cheek, in the East, answers exactly to our hearty shaking of hands between those of the same social station when meeting in familiar intercourse, and, if the Holy Spirit had been writing in our age and clime, instead of eighteen hundred years ago in the East, we may say, with all reverence, that He would have commanded believers to " salute one another with a holy shaking of hands ; " to meet, that is, as brethren of one rank before God, members of the same body, children of the same Father. " Let the brother who [is] low, glory in his exaltation ; but the rich in his humiliation."* Let it not be said that "*you* have dishonoured the poor man," or that "you have respect to persons."† This is the glorious truth contained in the words " salute one another with a holy kiss," which, like most of the deepest and strongest sayings of Scripture, convey instruction under a figurative rather than a literal form.

The main force here is in the word " one-

---

* James i. 9.     † James ii. 6, 9.

another." This may be well seen in the place
in the Epistle to the Romans where the injunction first occurs. A number of saluta-
tions, or ordinary messages of greeting, are
sent specially to certain men and women by
name, and, at the close of these, the apostle
adds, "salute one another," that is, "*all of
you*, men and women respectively, salute each
other" with the sign of friendliness and social
equality—"a kiss;" not as a mere act of
formal politeness, but rather with sincere
respect and affection—"a *holy* kiss."*

After I had written the above, happening
to look at Chrysostom's *Commentary on the
Romans*, I found this view so plainly and
simply stated, that I cannot do better than give
the words of "the golden-tongued preacher."
Commenting on Romans xvi. 16, "Salute
one another with a holy kiss," he says: "To
cast out of them, by this salutation, all arguing
that confused them [that is, all strife and
asperity], and all grounds for little pride ;
that neither the great might despise the
little, nor the little grudge at the great, but
that haughtiness and envy might be both
driven away, when this kiss soothed down

* Romans xvi. 16 ; and see 2 Corinthians xiii. 12.

and levelled every one. And therefore he
not only bids them salute in this way, but
sends in like manner to them the greeting even
of all the Churches. For 'there salute *you*,'
he says, not this or that person individually,
but 'the Churches of Christ.'" It was a
glorious sight, often to be witnessed in the
primitive Church—how seldom to be seen
now!—when some titled noble took his seat
below that of his own slave, in the secret
meeting-room, and humbly submitted to that
slave's instructions in the Way of Life.

Listen to the words of Lactantius, who
has been called, from his elegant and powerful style, the Cicero of the early Church.
They were perhaps written as late as the
year 300 A.D : "Some one will say, 'Are
there not among you some poor, and others
rich ; some servants, and others masters ?
Is there not some difference between individuals ?' There is none ; nor is there any
other cause why we mutually bestow upon
each other the name of 'brethren,' except
that we believe ourselves to be equal. For
since we measure all human things not by
the body, but by the spirit, although the
condition of bodies is different, yet we have

no servants, but we both regard and speak of them as brothers in spirit, in religion as fellow-servants. Riches also do not render men illustrious, except that they are able to make them more conspicuous by good works. For men are rich, not because they possess riches, but because they employ them on works of justice ; and they who seem to be poor, on this account are rich, because they are not in want and desire nothing. . . . God has consulted our interest in placing this in particular among the Divine precepts, ' He that exalts himself shall be abased, and he that humbles himself shall be exalted.'* And the wholesomeness of this precept teaches that he who shall [simply] place himself on a level with [other] men, and carry himself with humility, is esteemed excellent and illustrious in the sight of God. For the sentiment is not false which is brought forward in Euripides to this effect : ' The things which are here considered evil are esteemed good in heaven.' "†

Men's yearnings for a common brotherhood,

---

* Luke xiv. 11.
† Lactantius, "*Introduction to True Religion, or the Divine Institutions.*" Book v., chap. xvi.

where the strong artificial barriers which
human pride and selfishness have so success-
fully erected should be all broken down,
ought to be met to the full in the Church
of Christ—ought to be, but, alas! are not.
In those sections of it where this spirit of
levelling up, born of lowliness and love, is
strongest, there unquestionably is the largest
outpouring of the Spirit of God. We must
first "eagerly kiss the Son," or, in other words,
come to Jesus as suppliants for mercy, and
humbly and gratefully accept His salvation,
and submit to His authority, and then, with
the love of God shed abroad in our hearts, we
shall desire "to kiss one another"—that is, to
"love the *brotherhood*," manifesting our regard
for them by greeting them as one with ourselves, being "*in brotherly love* tenderly affec-
tioned *one to another; in honour* preferring *one
another*."* This word "tenderly-affectioned,"
φιλόστοργοι, *philostorgoi*, is one of almost
untranslatable force, being compounded of
terms signifying the affection of parents
for their children, or of animals for their
young, and it teaches us that the love of
believers for one another is to be warm and

* Romans xii. 10.

strong, like natural affection amongst near relations.

The general failure, throughout Christendom, to obey the meaning of this important apostolic command, has brought about, amongst the professing followers of Christ, a state of pride and worldliness destructive alike of holy love and spiritual life. With what trumpet tones has this been deplored and denounced, again and again, by the late generous and heroic General Gordon, whose whole life was a protest against it! Nor can it be doubted that such conduct, in the case of the larger part of the nominal Church, is leading to a reaction throughout civilised society, that threatens to overwhelm it in violent communistic and secular movements.

It is the great glory of the Bible, distinguishing it throughout from all other works of antiquity, that it realises " the dignity of man as man," and turns aside from the splendour of thrones and the palaces of the privileged few to deal with the fortunes of the humble poor. Dr. Geikie has well said, " In Egypt the masses were held in contempt by the great as ' the stinking multitude.' . . . In Asia, from the remotest times, even the high

officers of the sovereign have been content to
call themselves his slaves. . . . . In ancient
Greece, the citizens formed a privileged few—
the mass of their fellow-countrymen counted
for nothing ; and it was the same in Rome,
till citizenship was extended to all Italy, in
B.C. 90, after the Social War, to the unspeak-
able mortification of the great patrician party.
. . . In Scripture, however, there breathes a
higher spirit of liberty and respect to man.
Instead of giving pompous recitals of the
deeds of conquerors and kings, it follows the
history of simple patriarchs and their house-
holds. Amidst the slavish splendours of
Egypt, it dwells on the fortunes of a humble
shepherd tribe. That there be loyalty towards the One Living God is enough to raise
even the exiled Jacob to a prominence in it
that is not assigned to rank or power. It
enters the shepherd's tent ; it follows him in
his simple occupations ; it turns aside from
the palaces of Zoan to bend its regards on the
lowly inmates of the Hebrew slave-quarter
around. It sees no charm in the merely
outward and accidental ; the spiritual and
essential alone are valued. If these be found
on a throne, its occupant has corresponding

D

notice, but if they have retired to the tent or the slave-hut, they are followed thither, and the throne is passed by to reach them." *

But it was reserved for the gospel of the grace of God to reveal, in all its fulness, the true dignity and equality of redeemed man. Around Christ, His whole Church is gathered as one universal brotherhood, to whom a common ruin in sin, a common pardon through His blood, a common adoption amongst the sons and daughters of the Heavenly Father, and a common renewal by the same Holy Spirit, level all earthly distinctions of birth, rank, wealth, or intellect, and bring all alike into the fellowship of the saints, making them, in a word, " perfect in one." †

Nothing could be plainer than the burning words of the Master: " But *you* may not be called Rabbi ; for *one* is *your* Teacher ; and *all you* are *brethren.* And call no one your *father* upon earth ; for *one* is *your* Father, [even He] Who [is] in Heaven. Neither may you be called leaders [or chiefs] ; for *one* is *your* Leader [or Chief] [even] Christ. But *he that*

* *Hours with the Bible.* Vol. I., pp. 6, 7.
† John xvii. 23.

*is greatest among you* shall be *your* servant.
And *whosoever shall exalt himself* shall be
humbled ; and *whosoever shall humble himself*
shall be exalted."* The full force of this
important passage is much obscured in our
version. The " Teacher " alluded to is not
named in the best texts. But as believers
are to call only God the Father their " Father,"
and only Christ, God the Son, their "Leader, or
Chief," so the inference is that, when our Lord
says " *one* is *your* Teacher " (διδάσκαλος, *di-
daskalos*), without naming him, He means God
the Spirit, of Whom afterwards, when He
speaks of Him in private to His disciples, He
says, " *He* shall teach (διδάξει, *didaxei*) *you*
all things." Hence we learn from this text
that the Triune God is the only Father, Chief,
and Teacher of the disciples of Christ ; " the
only one," says Bishop Alford in his commentary on this verse, " in all these relations
on whom they can rest and depend." And
he immediately adds, " *They* (all believers)
*are brethren : all substantially equal—none by
office or precedence nearer to God than another ;
none standing between his brother and God.*"

* Matthew xxiii. 8—12. Some texts read in verse 10,
" for *your Leader* [or *Chief*] is one [even] Christ."

Again our Blessed Lord declares even more emphatically the same truth. "Ye know that *the rulers of the nations* lord it over them, and *their great ones* exercise authority over them. But it shall not be *so* among you ; but whosoever *of you* would become *great* shall be *your* servant (διάκονος, *diakonos*) ; and whosoever would be chief [or first] *among you* shall be *your* slave (δοῦλος, *doulos*) : Even as *the Son of Man* came not to be ministered unto, but to minister, and to give his life a ransom for many." *

Very clear, too, is the teaching of "the apostle of the Gentiles," "Be of *the same* mind *towards one another ;* set not your mind *on high things,* but take your part *with the lowly ;* " and again, " Submitting to one another in fear of Christ ; " and again, "In *humbleness of mind* esteeming *each other* better than yourselves." †   If, as believers, we cultivate this spirit of lowliness and love, we fulfil one of our Lord's latest wishes, and give the liveliest evidence of the truth of His Divine Mission ; for did not He pray, the night before He died, that we "may *all* be *one,* even as

* Matthew xx. 25—28.
† Romans xii. 16 ; Ephesians v. 21 ; Philippians ii. 3.

Thou, Father, art in Me, and I in Thee, . .
THAT THE WORLD MAY BELIEVE THAT THOU
HAST SENT ME!"*

It is sadly significant of the loss of this
truth that, throughout most sections of Christendom, men ignore the fact that the one
inspired scriptural title of the members of
Christ's Church, everywhere in use amongst
themselves in the apostolic age, as a term of
address, descriptive of their relation to one
another, is " Brethren." Five titles occur in
the New Testament. Strange to say, the one
most frequently employed now is that which
only occurs three times, and then, in each
instance, unmistakably as a nick-name, or
term of contempt, given by unbelieving Jews
and heathen Gentiles—namely, " Christian ! "
Thus we read, " the disciples were first called
' Christians ' at Antioch," † plainly in derision,
for never once do we find it used by one
believer to another, or in speaking of another,
or by the Holy Spirit of the Church. Agrippa
says, in evident mockery, possibly assumed to
hide an emotion of which he was ashamed,

---

* John xvii. 21. The words *"world," "thou,"* and *"me"*
are emphatic by their place in the last clause of this verse.
† Acts xi. 26.

"with *little* [*trouble*] art thou persuading [thy-
self] to make *me a 'Christian!'*"\* The only
other passage where the name occurs is equally
plain, and becomes very striking and forceful
when viewed in this light. The Apostle
Peter says, " Let not *any of you* suffer as a
murderer or a thief . . yet if *as a 'Christian'*
[any of you suffer] let him not be ashamed,"
that is, notwithstanding that he is arraigned
under this disgraceful name ! †

The title . that comes next in frequency,
the name " Believer," is found about twenty-
five times, and is employed as a fitting and
honourable description of the Lord's people.
The term " Saint," or rather " Saints," for it is
used in the plural in every instance but one,
comes next, occurring some sixty times, and
is applied in much the same way as the term
" Believer." ‡ The word " Disciple " is similarly used some ninety-six times in the New
Testament ; yet only as a designation, never
as a mode of address. These three titles, " Believers," " Saints," " Disciples," are given to the
Church in its relation to its Lord and Saviour.

But the one favourite and peculiar ap-

---

\* Acts xxvi. 28. See Revised Version. † 1 Peter iv. 15, 16.
‡ See Appendix F, on the Title of " Saint."

pellation, which occurs most constantly, is
"Brethren." In this style not only are members of the Church spoken of by one another,
but also personally addressed in both oral
and written communications. The name
"Brethren" is found in the Acts and the
Epistles about a hundred times, and the
singular "brother" thirty-three times more,
while the feminine form "sister," which occurs
six times,* appears to be the same technical name given to believing women. And
this word "Brethren" is everywhere employed
in the New Testament by the members of the
primitive Church, when addressing their fellow-
members, as essentially their own proper title,
expressive of the nature of their calling in
their relation to one another. †

* Romans xvi. 1 ; 1 Corinthians vii. 15 ; ix. 5 ; 1 Timothy
v. 2 ; James ii. 15 ; 2 John, 13.

† The words "Friends," "Heirs," "Children," and
some few more terms, either alone or in combination with
other expressions, occur, with some frequency, as applied to
believers, but always by way of figurative descriptions of
their character and privileges, rather than as recognised terms
of nomenclature. Perhaps "Beloved" should have been included in the list of names I have given above. It occurs
some 13 times, and in 12 out of the 13, like "Brother," it is
employed as a term of address. Seven times more we meet
with "Beloved" in connection with "brother," for the
former word expresses in a strong degree much the same
sense as the latter.

It is very interesting to notice that this was recognised by our Reformers, for the one title by which they have directed the minister to address the congregation at the morning and evening service of the Church of England, in the exhortation which forms the very first uninspired portion of that service, is "Brethren" —"Dearly beloved brethren." In all the other services of the Prayer Book the words of address are precisely similar, either " brethren," "dearly beloved," or "dearly beloved brethren," while the deceased member of the Church is called, in the Burial Service, " our brother " or " our sister."

Another most important aspect of the subject must not be passed over. The account given everywhere in the New Testament of the Church as one great brotherhood of saved men of all sorts and conditions gathered around Christ in perfect spiritual equality, children of one Father, fellow-servants of one Master, and taught, without any distinction, not only to regard one another as friends and equals, but even to esteem each other better than themselves, and to submit themselves one to another, in the very nature of things, utterly precludes the existence within that Church of a priestly caste!

Such a fundamental view of the *Ecclesia* (the " Church," or " Assembly," as the word means) positively and for ever settles this point, and razes to the ground the very stronghold of Anti-christ's superstition. It leaves no place or possibility for the lofty claims of a special sacerdotal class. "*One* is *your* Teacher, and ALL YOU are BRETHREN." ALL of you, without exception, as redeemed men, are "equal in dignity, in destiny, in privilege ; a spiritual republic, a theocratic family." But if, in the Church of Christ, one order of men had been set apart to offer up a sacrifice for the living and the dead, to hear the confessions and pronounce the absolution of the rest, to act as their sole judges and rulers, to stand as the indispensable mediators between God and man, to be clothed, in a word, with far more powers and privileges than were bestowed on the Jewish, or claimed by the Pagan, priesthood, surely, instead of Believers being commanded to "salute one another with a holy kiss," as being all alike on one perfect spiritual equality, they would have been commanded to kiss the hand of the priest, in token of the lowliest submission !

Here, in the last place, we are led to right

views of the ministry.  SERVICE, not RULE, is
its distinguishing feature.  It has been well
said, " The officers of a Christian Church are
simply a body of men who are willing to
become their brethren's ministers [that is,
servants]—to take upon themselves additional
labours and responsibilities for their brethren's
benefit, which they are not bound, otherwise
than through love, to perform.  And the cha-
racteristics of a Christian minister, ideally considered, are humility and kindness and self-
denial.  The whole worth and significance of
his service is that it be done for the society's
sake and not for his own.  Having no interests
to seek, but some to renounce ; finding his
wages mainly in his work ; denying himself
for the sake of others, and desiring not to be
ministered unto, but to minister ; superior to
his brethren only because more like his Lord,
and honourable only in virtue of his humbleness—such is a Christian minister."  These
are, in the main, noble words—as true as they
are noble.

It follows of necessity—would it were more
generally realised !—that a minister is not
constituted the sole authorised teacher of the
Church, and that much less is he appointed to

be "lording it over *the great assigned portion*
[of God]," that is "the Church,"* above all in
matters of "faith," but that, on the contrary,
his true place is to be one of their "*joyful
fellow-workers.*" For the Apostle, speaking
of the very highest order of ministry, even
that of Apostles themselves, says, "not that
we have lordship over *your* faith, but are your
*joyful fellow-workers.*" † The emphasis I have
marked here by italics is given very plainly
by the order of the words in the Greek
original. ‡

That the expression, rendered in our version in its naked literalness, "helpers [or
rather, fellow-workers] of your joy," should
be translated "your *joyful fellow-workers,*" I

* 1 Peter v. 3. See Appendix G, on the Great Assigned
Portion.

† 2 Corinthians i. 24. The word I have translated "*fellow-
workers,*" συνεργοί, *sunergoi*, has, for its chief or first sense,
that of "working together with," "joining or helping in
work ;" sometimes it means "an accomplice." Its marked
technical, second meaning is, "one of the same trade or
labour as another," a "fellow-workman." It is in this
last technical sense that the Apostle, in his figurative and
vigorous style, appears to use it here, where, as spoken of the
Brethren, drawn mostly, as we are expressly told they were,
from the working classes (1 Corinthians i. 26—28), in a great
trade centre like Corinth, it would be particularly effective.

‡ See Appendix H, on the Emphasis on "Your" and
"Fellow-workers" in 2 Corinthians i. 24.

think there can be little doubt. "From the hands of a man of his brother" is "from the hands of his *brother* man ;"\* "home of thy righteousness" is "thy *righteous* home ;"† "mountain of my holiness" is "my *holy* mountain ;"‡ "God of my righteousness" is "my *righteous* God ;"§ "city of his strength" is "his '*strong*' city ;"‖ "images of thy silver" is "thy *silver* images ;"¶ "throne of His glory" is "His *glorious* throne ;"\*\* "the might of His glory" is "His *glorious* might ;"†† "in the body of his flesh" is "in his *fleshly* body ;"‡‡ "the mind of his flesh" is "his *fleshly* mind ;"§§ "holiness of the truth" is "the *true* holiness ;"‖‖ "angels of His power" is "His *powerful* angels ;"¶¶ "the body of our humiliation" is "our *humiliated* or *humbled* body ;" and "the body of His glory" is "His *glorious* body,"\*\*\* together with a great number of other instances that might be cited from the New Testament. "Fellow-workers of your joy"

---

\* Genesis ix. 5.
† Job viii. 6.
‡ Psalm ii. 6.
§ Psalm iv. 1.
‖ Proverbs x. 15.
¶ Isaiah xxx. 22.
\*\* Matthew xix. 28.

†† Colossians i. 11 ; see also Ephesians i. 12.
‡‡ Colossians i. 22.
§§ Colossians ii. 18.
‖‖ Ephesians iv. 24.
¶¶ 2 Thessalonians i. 7.
\*\*\* Philippians iii. 21.

is, therefore, on the face of it, likely to be
"your *joyful fellow-workers.*" *

This being the "*joyful fellow-workers*" of
the Church of God implies labouring in the
humblest offices on behalf of and side by side
with other believers, and calling upon and
encouraging them to exercise to the full their
own gifts and graces for the furtherance of
the Master's cause. May the Lord raise up
and send forth into His vineyard many such
ministers!

But, perhaps, some will exclaim, " Do you
mean to deny the rule of the ministerial
office? Would you deprive Bishops, Pres-
byters,† and Deacons of the authority con-
ferred upon them by the teaching of the

---

* See Appendix I, on the Emphasis on "Fellow" and
"Joyful" in 2 Corinthians i. 24, for the full proof of this
point.

† The word "priest" is the πρεσβύτερος, *presbuteros,* or
"elder," of the New Testament, an office modelled on the
eldership of the synagogue, and having nothing to do with the
functions of a sacrificing priest, the Greek for which is ἱερεύς,
*hiereus,* and the Latin *sacerdos.* This word "elder," *presbuteros,* from the Low Latin form *presbyter,* and the old
French form *prestre* (now *prêtre*), became our "priest," as
may be seen from any good English dictionary. Where
"priest," therefore, occurs in the Prayer Book, spoken of a
minister of the Church of England, it stands simply as the
English form of the New Testament word *presbuteros,* or
"elder."

Apostles?" I hasten to answer, "No." On the contrary, I would arm them with a power and authority of Divine appointment and invincible strength. In these lawless times, when the bonds of discipline within and around the Church are all loosening, I would point faithful ministers to the adequate and only means of attaining to a spiritual rule, strong with all the strength of Christ.

The authority of ministers of the Gospel is not the same as that of civil rulers. It is founded not on force, but on fidelity. It stands not in their office itself, but in their faithful discharge of it. It is not upheld by any temporal or spiritual power belonging to their order, but by the esteem and affection of their faithful flocks. Above all, its greatness is measured by the depth to which it stoops. This is one of the numerous paradoxes of Divine Grace, well-known to that " able minister of the New Covenant " who said, " When I am weak, then am I *powerful.*"* In this way it is true of ministry, as of all else in the kingdom of heaven, "*whosoever shall desire to save his life* will lose it, and *whosoever shall lose his life for my sake* will find it."†

* 2 Corinthians xii. 10.    † Matthew xvi. 25.

Let me repeat the plain words in which the Master Himself has stated this important truth. "Ye know that *the rulers of the nations* lord it over them, and *their great ones* exercise authority over them. But it shall not be *so* among you ; but whosoever *of you* would become *great* shall be *your* servant (διάκονος, *diakonos*) ; and whosoever would be chief [or first] *among you* shall be *your* slave (δοῦλος, *doulos*). Even as *the Son of Man* came not to be ministered unto, but to minister, and to give His life a ransom for many." *

Here we have, in a single sentence, the secret of all rank, dignity, and rule, in the Church of Christ. Let us take, as a commentary on these words of our blessed Lord, those of the Apostle Paul in that chapter which he commences by claiming respect for his office—"Let a man *so* account *of us* as officers [literally, 'under-rowers'] of Christ. . . . We [are] fools for Christ's sake, but you [are] wise in Christ ; we [are] weak, but you [are] mighty ; you [are] glorious, but we [are] unhonoured ;" and then, after a list of the deepest humiliations and privations which he, in common with the other Apostles, is suffer-

* Matthew xx. 25, 28.

ing in consequence of faithful ministerial labours, he concludes, " I beseech you, therefore, become *imitators of me.*" *

In every passage where ministerial authority is spoken of in the Epistles, it is sanctioned on the ground of ministerial worthiness. Take the following instances. " Remember those who had the rule over you, who spoke *to you* the word of God, *of whose life, attentively considering the issue* [*or end*], imitate their faith." † These words, spoken of the martyred ministers of the " Hebrews " [that is, the Palestine Jews], men such as Stephen and James, urge respect for their past rule on the plea of their faithful example. Again, of living ministers, it is said in the same chapter, " Obey those who have the rule over you, and submit [yourselves], for *they* watch on behalf of your souls, as those who must give *account*, that they may do *this with joy* and not with groaning." ‡ Who would not reverence and follow such ministers as these? Yet our allegiance is claimed not because of their office itself, but because of their high unselfish labours in its discharge. The Apostle, addressing the Thessalonian

* 1 Cor. iv. 1, 10—16. † Hebrews xiii. 7. ‡ Hebrews xiii. 17.

Church, says, " Now we beseech you, brethren,
to know [that is, to duly regard] those labouring among you, and presiding over you
in [the] Lord, and admonishing you, and to
esteem them very highly with love for their
work's sake."* What could be plainer than
this? Our "due regard" and "esteem" are
not claimed for the sake of their office, but for
the sake of their "work."

Once more the Apostle enjoins, "Let *the
elders that preside well* be counted worthy *of
ample maintenance*, especially those who labour
in preaching and in teaching." † The words,
in our version, "counted worthy of *double
honour*," mean plainly, "counted worthy of
*ample maintenance*," "double" being a Hebrew
expression for "large" or "ample,"‡ and
" honour " for " honorarium," that is, " gift "
or "maintenance."§ But it is only those

* 1 Thessalonians v. 12.

† 1 Timothy v. 17. It is literally "in word (ἐν λόγῳ, *en
logō*) and teaching;" but "word" is thus used in several
places for "preaching" the gospel (Luke i. 2; Acts vi. 2;
Acts x. 44), and evidently stands for this here.

‡ 2 Kings ii. 9; Job xi. 6; Isaiah xl. 2; Revelation
xviii. 6.

§ Thus Paul says of the grateful people at Malta that
" they honoured us with many honours," that is, "liberally
presented us with *many presents*," adding, "and *when we
departed*, they laded us with such things as were necessary "

E

elders who "*preside well*" who are to be thus
cared for; and a very strong and special
emphasis is thrown on this word "*well*"
by its having virtually the first place in the
sentence.  Here, as in all other cases, the
claim of ministers to the regard of the rest of
the Church is not grounded upon their public
office, but on their personal character.  And
that character, to make them "great," must be
one of lowliness and self-abasement.  For
"whosoever *of you* would become *great* shall be
*your* servant; and whosoever would be chief
[or first] *among you* shall be *your* slave." *

This is the indispensable condition if
officers of the Church would obtain spiritual

(Acts xxviii. 10).  Our Lord says, "and honour not his
father and mother," or, as better authorities read, "he shall
not honour his father," which, in this connection, plainly
means "and maintain not his father and mother," or "he
shall not maintain his father" (Matthew xv. 6).  And in
this same chapter, "honour *widows* who are [really] widows,"
as we gather from the following verse, evidently means,
"maintain *widows* who are [really] widows." (1 Timothy
v. 3.) A present, in the East, is a mark of honour, for
rulers and great men must always be approached with an
offering as part of the respect paid to their rank.  The *back-
sheesh*, or present, for which an Arab clamours, is valued not
only for the sake of the money itself, but also for the honourable nature of such an acknowledgment.  Hence the similar
meaning of the words "honour" and "gifts."

* Matthew xx. 26, 27.

power, and all its loyal members should earnestly pray that they may comply with it. Those who do will have no need to assert or defend their authority. It will be manifest to all men by the Master's mark.

# APPENDIX A.

## FELLAHHEEN AND SEPHARDEEM.

A *FELLAHH* is a peasant, or agriculturist, answering to our small farmer, farm-labourer, and village inhabitant generally. There are, as there were in Bible times, just three conditions of life in Palestine; the *Belladeen*, or "dwellers in walled towns," mostly merchants, tradesmen, and artisans, who have lived there for generations, usually in their own freehold houses; the *Fellahheen*, or "ploughmen," who dwell in settled unwalled villages, and are joint freehold owners of the soil, or rather of the right to cultivate all the lands of each village in common; and the *Bedaween*, or nomad Arabs, who roam the deserts in and around the country, dwelling in tents, or, as they call them, "houses of hair," and whose only occupation, besides indiscriminate robbery, is that of shepherds and herdsmen. Each of these three conditions of life differs from the others as to dress and social habits. The *Bedaween* are the least civilised; the *Fellahheen* are more advanced in the arts of life; while the *Belladeen*, who have many luxuries and comforts to which the other two are strangers, look down upon both of them as from a lofty height. The *Fellahheen* class form the bulk of the population in Bible lands. Those in Palestine are thought, on many grounds, to be the descendants of the original nations of Canaan. Their manners and customs are exceedingly simple, and are evidently of hoary antiquity.

The Jews in Palestine are divided into three principal classes : the *Sephardeem*, or true Eastern Jews, who came to Syria from Spain, when cruelly banished from the latter country some 400 years ago, who talk ancient Spanish and Arabic, and observe Oriental customs ; the *Askenazeem*, or German-speaking Jews, Germans being thought by the Jews to be the descendants of Askenaz (Genesis x. 3), a comparatively recent emigration from central Europe, and the *Moograbeen*, or South-Western Jews, that is, those who have long settled in the north of Africa.

## APPENDIX B.

### EMPHASIS IN BIBLICAL HEBREW AND GREEK.

THE 'question of emphasis in the Hebrew and Greek originals of Holy Scripture, though it has been generally overlooked, is a very interesting and important one. There are three chief ways in which this special force has been given ; a force, let it be carefully observed, which not only lends nervous strength and beauty to the style of the inspired writers, but serves at times to explain their meaning. These ways are—(1) by the position of words or phrases in a sentence ; (2) by the figure of Repetition, expressed or understood, of which there are, in Hebrew alone, more than forty subtle and beautiful varieties ; (3) by grammatical construction.

Want of space permits me to do little more
than enumerate these three principal divisions, and
renders it absolutely necessary to pass over the
very numerous particulars that occur under each.
I must, therefore, dismiss the second and third
heads with this remark, to which I would especially
call the attention of all diligent students of the
Bible, that—as the Greek of the New Testament
was written by Jews, at home in the idioms and
expressions of the Hebrew Scriptures, and in the
very literal renderings of those idioms and expressions in the Septuagint—countless instances
naturally occur of a force foreign to classical
Greek, but very familiar to Hebrew, throughout
the pages of the Gospels, Acts, Epistles, and
Revelation.

As, however, the first of these three heads is
that which supplies by far the most frequent
examples—certainly the bulk of those that are to
be found in this work—and has been strangely
overlooked by scholars, a further word of explanation seems necessary. It must be remembered
that the New Testament is written in what may
be called Biblical Greek. By Biblical Greek I
mean the Greek of the Septuagint. The Septuagint, as is well known, is a Greek translation of
the Old Testament, made at Alexandria 285 years
before Christ, and which, in our Saviour's time,
had become, throughout the world, the Authorised
Version of that day, from which the writers of the
New Testament generally quote. "The Septuagint," says the writer under that head in Dr.

Smith's *Dictionary of the Bible*, "is the mould in
which the thoughts and expressions of the Apostles
and Evangelists are cast. In this version Divine
truth has taken the Greek language as its shrine,
and adapted it to the things of God."

Now, in Biblical Greek, each of the different
parts of speech has its own proper place in a
sentence, and, when put in an earlier position,
becomes emphatic. For instance, the verb uniformly precedes its subject, object, or adverbial
qualification. Thus, in the Septuagint, the order
of the words is as follows :—"And saw God the
light " (Genesis i. 4), "And called God the light
day " (Genesis i. 5), for " God saw the light," and
" God called the light day." This is the proper and
constant order, and there is, therefore, no emphasis. But in Genesis i. 2 the order of the Greek
is, " And *the Spirit of God* moved," &c., where the
subject, " *the Spirit of God*," being put before the
verb "moved," makes the former emphatic ; and,
on turning to the Hebrew Bible, these words will
be seen to occupy the same position and to possess
the same force. Again, in Biblical Greek, adverbs
uniformly follow the verbs that they qualify. But
where an adverb precedes a verb it becomes
emphatic. Thus, in the same chapter of the
Septuagint, the opening verse of Genesis runs,
"*At first* created God the heavens and the earth."
In this way emphasis is thrown on the words "*At
first*," an emphasis which they are found to possess
in the Hebrew original. In like manner adjectives
and possessive pronouns ordinarily follow the

substantives they qualify, the subject of the verb precedes the object, &c. &c., and where these positions are reversed there is emphasis. Now all this is just the same in the Biblical Greek of the New Testament as in the Biblical Greek of the Septuagint.

The Holy Spirit has, in this way, constantly given to certain words and phrases a strong force, which is altogether lost in the various excellent translations. Rotherham's *New Testament Critically Emphasised*, published by Messrs. Bagster and Co., an exceedingly literal English Version from the text of Tregelles, is an able attempt to mark every instance where such emphasis occurs—in the case of the New Testament.

In Biblical Hebrew, the order of words in a sentence is, if anything, even more regular than in Biblical Greek, owing to the greater simplicity of its primitive forms; and, by the inversion of this order, the Old Testament has been made to abound with a similar emphasis, which, as far as I am aware, has not as yet been reproduced in any English translation. And here let me say that Hebrew has one great advantage over Greek, or, indeed, any other Western tongue, as a language of Revelation. Its poetry has no rhythm, or measured feet. The nature and beauty of Hebrew verse consist in the use of choice words, figures of speech, and ideas; exceeding brevity and simplicity; and, chiefly, in a parallelism of thought, expressive of agreement or contrast, in many regular forms. It has been well called "thought rhythm," and its great excellence has been pointed out, in that *it loses less than any other kind of poetry by translation.* To this let me add what I believe has not been remarked before, that *it preserves by its simple form the exact order of words in a sentence, thus exhibiting emphasis as plainly as prose,* which no poetry that depends on metre can possibly do, for the exigencies of rhythmical measure always require an arbitrary and irregular arrangement of words. The reader will observe this in the passages given in these pages from such poems as the Psalms and the prophecies of Isaiah. A delicate but exquisite power is thus imparted to these poetical compositions, which will be sought for in vain in any others. The Hebrew student who reads them in this light will find a new world of beauty, and so will the English reader when possessed of a translation which brings them into view.

Wherever emphasis has been laid, in any of the above ways, on the words of either the Old or New Testament which are quoted in this work, I have shown it by placing such words in italics, while, to avoid confusion, words that are added to the text to make the meaning clearer, I have placed, by way of distinction, in square brackets. There are as many as three or four shades, or degrees, of emphasis in Biblical Hebrew and Greek ; but as very special and unusual marks would have been needed to distinguish these, I have contented myself in this work, for the most part, with noting the *fact* of emphasis rather than its *degree.*

Let me add that this subject of emphasis is especially worthy of the attention of all who read the Bible in public, and who should, in such reading, give emphasis by their voice to those words which have been rendered emphatic by the Holy Spirit.

---

## APPENDIX C.

### THE LOGICAL CONCORD.

IN Proverbs xxiv. 26

" [*The*] *two lips* [*each of them*] shall kiss
That which returns [an answer of] straightforward words,"

owing to the word "*lips*" being in the dual number — that is, "*two lips*" — and the word "shall kiss" in the singular, it has been concluded that there could be no concord between them, and that therefore "*lips*" must be the object and not the subject of the verb. But countless anomalies of this kind teach the careful Hebrew scholar that, as to *outward form*, there is no absolute necessity for agreement in gender, number, or even person, between a subject and its verb, either in that primitive tongue or in any of its cognates, Arabic, Syriac, &c. That such agreement is the rule, there can be no doubt; but the exceptions are numerous, and may all be clearly accounted for by a simple and interesting principle laid down by Dr. Lee in his Hebrew Grammar—namely, that of the logical concord.*

* Dr. Lee's *Grammar of the Hebrew Language*, Second Ed., pp. 274—280.

A good illustration of the logical, as distinguished from the formal, concord is furnished by a passage very similar to the verse in question. This passage, which contains precisely the same construction as Proverbs xxiv. 26, but, unlike that text, stands in the main rightly rendered in our Authorised Version, is literally—

> "[*The*] *two lips of the wise* [*the whole or each of them*] it keeps them." *

The *formal* concord would require the verb to be in the plural ("keep") to agree with the subject "*two lips;*" but instead of this, it is in the third person singular ("keeps"), and a true *logical* concord is supplied by the words, understood but not expressed, "*the whole or each of them.*" Here let me add my increasing conviction (I am not aware that this idea has been pointed out before) that, wherever any of the ordinary formal concords are broken, the ruggedness thus produced, the pause to supply the words (implied though not expressed) that make the logical concord complete, and, above all, *the repetition, in another form, of the subject in these implied words*, convey in Eastern languages a marked and striking emphasis. For instance, this implied expression, "*the whole or each of them,*" is

---

* Proverbs xiv. 3. The verb here is in the third person singular, תִּשְׁמוֹרֵם, *tishmooraim*, "it keeps them." In order that the reader may understand the full force of the bold and striking figure by which the "*two lips*"—that is, when prudently used in guarded and godly speech—are said "to keep" the wise, he is referred to the explanation of the peculiar Eastern office of "the Keeper" given in my *Palestine Explored*, Second Edition, p. 209. Messrs. J. Nisbet & Co.

a repetition in other words of the subject "*two lips*," and, as I hope shortly to show in another work, in all such cases of repetition, in tongues of the Hebrew group, a strong emphasis is given.

---

## APPENDIX D.

### THE TAHLEEL, OLOOLEH, OR WOOLWAL.

THE word "yell," used by James in the passage "Come now, you rich, weep and yell" (James v. 1), ὁλολύζοντες, *ololuzontes*, the *ululo* of the Romans, and *ullaloo* cry of the Irish wake, is the Arab *olooleh*—the prolonged, tremulous shriek of distress and excitement, which is such a peculiar feature of the East. It is generally confined to the women, though sometimes uttered by men, as, for instance, by Bedaween, Koords, and Circassians, as a war cry, when it may be heard, as our troops in the Soudan must have often heard it, high above the din of battle, rousing these savage warriors to the utmost pitch of frenzy. It resembles the yell of a jackal, but is far louder and longer sustained. It is made by rapid vibrations of the tongue against the palate, aided by a movement of the four fingers of the hand upon the mouth. The principal Arabic name for it is *tahleel*, but it is also called *ziraleet* or *zughareet*, *woolwal*, and *olooleh*, the last because this shrill and terribly piercing cry sounds like *olooleh*, or *lill, lill*, constantly and quickly repeated.

The women use this "yell" on all occasions of unwonted excitement, whether of joy or grief. But it stands very specially connected with lamentation and hopeless woe. It is always raised by the females of a family, and by the professional mourning women (Jeremiah ix. 17), with awful suddenness, the instant a death takes place. The Evangelist Mark tells us, in the graphic style so characteristic of his Gospel, that, when our Lord reached the ruler of the synagogue's house, just after his little daughter had breathed her last, they were "weeping and yelling [that is, raising the *tahleel* or *olooleh*] greatly" (Mark v. 38). The word here, ἀλαλάζοντας, *alalazontas*, is only another form of the word *ololuzontes* used in James v. 1.

This *tahleel*, or *woolwal* (the Arabic form of the Hebrew *yalyal*, a structure of the verb *yalal*), is, unquestionably, the meaning of the similar Hebrew verb לל, *yalal*. As this verb *yalal* is the only one rendered "howl" in our version of the Old Testament, and, most fortunately, is uniformly so rendered in each of the twenty-nine places where it occurs, the English reader may note its special force in every instance. There are also two Hebrew nouns from this root, *yĕlail* and *yelalah*, both always rendered in our version "howling" —the only words there that are so rendered. Our English word "yell" comes from this Hebrew root, *yalal*, "to raise the cry of *olooleh*." *Yalal* is always used in the Old Testament as an accompaniment of lamentation and woe.

## THE KISS OF PEACE.

THIS monograph would not be complete without a notice of the mistake made on the subject of "the kiss of peace" by the writer of the article "Kiss," in Smith's *Dictionary of Christian Antiquities.* This author declares that "no limitation is expressed or implied. . . . nor is there any doubt that the primitive usage was for the 'holy kiss' to be given promiscuously, without any restriction as to sexes or ranks, among those who were all one in Christ Jesus. . . . In the frequent allusions to the kiss of peace which occur in the early Christian worship, (*sic*) there is no reference to any restriction." The fact that the passage I have given from the *Apostolical Constitutions*, Book ii., chap. lvii., referred by Canon Westcott to the third century, expressly limits this kiss to the salutation of men with men only, and women with women only, shows how cautious one has to be in accepting even the most confident statements in the best books of reference !

The writer in question gives the words of Athenagoras, in his *Plea (or Embassy) for the Christians*, who, quoting apparently from some Apocryphal book, says, "for the Logos (the Word) again says to us 'if any one kiss a second time because it has given him pleasure [he sins],'" and adds, "Therefore the kiss, or rather the salutation, should be given with the greatest care, since, if there be mixed with it the least defilement of thought, it excludes us from eternal life" (*Legat. pro Christian*, chap. xxxii). But all who, like myself, have lived in the East, or who know from the classics the nameless vice to which the heathen were, and still are, so awfully addicted, will at once perceive that this is not necessarily any reference at all to a salutation between the two sexes.

Again, he quotes from the *Instructor* (*Pædagogus*) of Clement of Alexandria a passage the chief point of which he appears to overlook. It is one on Love and the need of its being genuine. Clement says, "If we are called to the kingdom of God, let us walk worthy of the kingdom, loving God and our neighbour. But love is not tested by a kiss, but by kindly feeling. But there are those that do nothing but make the churches resound with a kiss, not having love itself within. For this very thing, the shameless use of the kiss, which ought to be mystic, occasions foul suspicions and evil reports. The Apostle calls the kiss holy" (*Pædagogus*, Book iii., chap. xi.). Here the main object is to warn against insincere greetings. What is said as to their noisy, ostentatious character giving rise to "foul suspicions" is entirely met by my reply to the last quotation. That it can have nothing to do with an exchange of greeting between a man and a woman, may be seen from the fact that Clement has said just before in the same chapter, on the subject of going to church worship, "Let the woman observe this further. Let her be entirely covered unless she happen to be at home.

. . . For this is the wish of the Word, since it is becoming for her to pray veiled." The writer of the article " Kiss," to whom I have alluded, *entirely leaves out this important statement that the women's faces were not to be even seen during Divine worship !*

This writer further adds that "the earliest example " of the distinction between the sexes is in the *Apostolical Constitutions*, and proceeds to quote from the *eighth* book the following words : " Let the deacon say to all, ' Salute ye one another with the holy kiss ;' and let the Clergy salute the Bishop, and the men of the laity salute the men, and the women the women " (*Apostolical Constitutions*, Book viii., chap. ii.). But this eighth book, which is of much later date than the first seven, probably came into existence considerably after the *real* " earliest example " which I have given from the second book—namely, " let the men salute one another, and the women one another, with the kiss in the Lord " ( *Apostolical Constitutions*, Book ii., chap. lvii.), and which the writer of the article in question has kept entirely out of sight.

In this passage, it will be observed, we have nothing about any distinction between the clergy and laity, as in the subsequent times of greater priestly assumption when the eighth book was penned. It is true that the *Apostolical Constitutions* is a work which shows, throughout, the marks of later corruptions and interpolations, is far from being a pure or Scriptural production, and is unquestionably a forgery in professing to be derived from the teaching of the Apostles. But, such as it is, it affords the first and only explicit statement as to those by whom the "kiss of peace" was given and received; and that one explicit statement of antiquity completely confirms the view which I have laboured to establish.

To later authors there is no occasion to refer, as the practice of the first three or four centuries is all that we need to know. Yet I think it right to state that, as far as my time would permit, I have diligently searched the whole of the Greek and Latin so-called Fathers, in Migne's series of two hundred and sixteen thick quarto volumes, and, still more carefully, the twenty-four volumes of Messrs. T. and T. Clark's series of the Ante-Nicene Christian Library, without finding any other passage to throw light on this question. Tertullian has a short chapter on "the kiss of peace" in his treatise "On Prayer" (De Oratione, chap. xviii.); but it gives no hint of this kiss passing between the different sexes.

The only passage that seems at all doubtful is one in Tertullian's piece entitled "*Ad Uxorem*," "To [my] Wife," where, warning her against the restraints and hindrances which a believing woman would encounter if married to a heathen, he asks, "For who would suffer his wife for the sake of visiting the brethren (*visitandorum fratrum*) to go round from street to street to others', and, indeed, to all the poorer, cottages? Who will willingly bear her being taken from his side by nocturnal convoca-

F

tions [Evening Services] if need be so? Who, finally, will, without anxiety, endure her spending a night out at the paschal solemnities? Who will, without some suspicion of his own, dismiss her to attend that Lord's feast (*convivium dominicum*) which they defame? Who will suffer her to creep into prison to kiss a martyr's bonds? Again, even to meet any one of the brethren to exchange the kiss?" ("*jam vero alicui fratrum ad osculum convenire*"). But here the word *fratrum*, "brethren," may, and probably should, be taken in the same general sense in which the word is used in the New Testament, to refer to believing women as well as men, and, in this particular instance, to mean women alone, the only portion of "the brethren." whom a pious married woman would, in the nature of things, be meeting to kiss. For surely a woman's going round to other houses "for the sake of visiting the brethren," would mean, for the sake of visiting other female members of the Church; and if this is the sense of "brethren" in one sentence, why not in another immediately following? The general drift of the whole passage is that a heathen husband would be impatient of his wife's having friends, pursuits, and engagements, all outside his own circle, and amongst the despised and hated "Christians."

The view taken of "the kiss of peace" in that excellent work, Fairbairn's *Imperial Bible Dictionary*, also shows a plain misconception. The writer there of the article "Kiss" says: "In the

early Church, and in consequence probably of
the extraordinary outburst of affection called forth
by the circumstances of the time, coupled with the
fervid temperament of the East, the kiss came into
use among the Christian brotherhood as a token
of relationship and mutual endearment in a
spiritual sense ; hence the exhortations in some
of the Epistles to salute one another with a holy
kiss." But, so far from this kiss being the mark
of anything " extraordinary," or a special out-of-
the-way token of " relationship in a spiritual sense,"
it was simply the ordinary social greeting among
friends and equals, commanded to be exchanged
by members of the Church in token of their true
fellowship, and as a recognition of their equality
in Christ. The terms " holy " and " loving," applied to this salutation, lift it, indeed, above the
level of coldness and worldly formality, and imply
that, amongst believers, it was to be a kind, sincere,
hearty greeting. But the kiss itself was, as I have
clearly shown, one of the ordinary usages of polite
society.

The care that is needed in reading the most
important works of reference may be still further
seen from the fact that, under the article " Kiss " in
the very large and valuable *Cyclopedia of Biblical,
Theological, and Ecclesiastical Literature*, edited by
Messrs. J. M. McClintock and J. Strong, the
following sentence occurs, " It was usual to kiss
the mouth (Genesis xxxiii. 4 ; Exodus iv. 27 ;
xviii. 7 ; 1 Samuel xx. 41 ; Proverbs xxiv. 26);"
yet, will my readers believe it, there is no hint in

the original of the kiss being given on the mouth in any one of these five alleged proof texts! The Hebrew, in the case of the first four, is simply "kissed," and refers, as I have shown above, to kissing the cheek, and in one case the hand (see pages 10, 37, 41); and the last alludes to greeting a document and not a person (see pages 19, 20).

---

## APPENDIX F.

### THE TITLE OF "SAINT."

THE title "saint," as applied to members of the Church, is used in the plural, with one single exception, each of the sixty times it occurs. The one exception is Philippians iv. 21, and even this may be said to be only an apparent exception. The expression in this verse is "every saint," and the word "every" here, πάντα, *panta*, has the sense of "all" or "the whole," and gives, as it were, this plural sense inherent in itself, to the noun "saint," which it is used to qualify. The expression is, therefore, equivalent to "all and each of the saints," or "the whole of the saints."

Not only is this the case with the substantive form "saint" or "holy one," but also with the precisely similar form when used as the adjective "holy." In the New Testament, three, and *only three*, individual persons are spoken of or to *by name* with the adjectival prefix "holy," and these are the Three Persons of the Divine Trinity, either separately or viewed as one—"Holy Father" (John xvii. 11), "Thy *Holy* Son [or Servant] Jesus" (Acts iv. 27, 30), "The Holy Spirit" (Matthew i. 18), and "*Holy, Holy, Holy*, Lord God Almighty" (Revelation iv. 8). This fact, like the former, is not a little significant.

The Romish practice of giving to human individuals the title of "Saint" is, like all other practices of that system of Antichrist, entirely opposed to the letter and spirit of Scripture. In the New Testament, no believer is spoken of in any other way than by the mention of his one name, or by the addition, at the end of that name, of his parentage, calling, nationality, party, or simple membership with the Church. Even in the case of Apostles,—"Paul," "Peter," "John," "James," is all that we find in any Scriptural reference to an individual believer, except when, for the sake of distinction, we find such terms as "Simon son of Jonah" (Matthew xvi. 17), "James the [son] of Zebedee" (Matthew x. 2), "Matthew the tax-collector" (Matthew x. 3), "Luke the beloved physician" (Colossians iv. 14), "Trophimus the Ephesian" (Acts xxi. 29), "Simon the Cananæan, or Zealot" (Matthew x. 4, see Luke vi. 15, Acts i. 13), "Quartus the brother" (Romans xvi. 23), &c. Indeed, as if carefully to guard against the error, afterwards to arise in the Church, of giving this special title to certain believers, and thus treating them as belonging to an order holier than the rest, *the word "saint" is never used except in the plural, or in speaking of the Church as a body, and the word "holy," which is the meaning of "saint," is never conjoined with any other name than that of God.*

It is much to be regretted that the Church of England, at the time of the Reformation, retained the Romish practice of speaking of the Apostles and Evangelists as "Saint Paul," "Saint John," &c. ; for it is an unscriptural practice, and ONE UN-KNOWN TO THE EARLY CHURCH. This may be seen by a reference to any of its writers of the first three centuries whose works have come down to our time. Every one of these works has now been carefully translated into English, in *The Ante-Nicene Christian Library* (published by Messrs. T. and T. Clark, Edinburgh, in 24 volumes), and may therefore be consulted by all.

It is perhaps to be still more regretted that our Revisers, in their Version of the New Testament, have placed the letter " S." before the names of the four Evangelists in the titles of the four Gospels, and again before that of John in the second title of the Revelation. It is, alas ! especially significant that the letter "S." *alone* is used. The old-fashioned " St." stands for the English word "Saint," while " S." stands for the Latin word " Sanctus," and it is not a little sad to find that this Latinizing, Ritualistic innovation, has been stamped on our Revised Version. But neither the letter " S." nor the letters " St." have any right to stand where our Revisers have placed the former.

In the list of " Readings and Renderings pre-ferred by the American Committee recorded at their desire," at the end of the Revised Version of the New Testament, at the head of all, occurs this necessary emendation, "Strike out 'S.' (*i.e.*, Saint) from the title of the Gospels, and from the heading of the pages." * Nor could they consistently have failed to protest against its insertion. In no ancient manuscript is the word "Saint" found in any of these titles, and every one of the Revisers must have been well aware that there is not the faintest reason for supposing that it ever formed part of the original text ! That they should have gone out of their way to insert or permit the insertion of this unauthorised term is the more lamentable because it is just what, in the preface to this version, they distinctly declared they would not do. After enumerating the Principles and Rules agreed to by the Committee of Convocation, on May the 25th, 1870, as those upon which the Revision was to be made, they add, "these rules it has been our endeavour faithfully and consistently to follow." Yet rule four, which they quote just above, says that "the text to be adopted be that for which the evidence is decidedly preponderating," while, as I have now shown, there was no evidence whatever for the insertion of this "S." It is sadly calculated to be a stumbling-block to the unlearned, and is an act unworthy of Protestant translators.

All who wish to be Scriptural, and to follow the well-known practice of the Primitive Church, should

---

* They seem to have overlooked the fact that the letter "S." has also been wrongly inserted in the title of the Revelation.

be very careful in referring to the Apostles, the Evangelists, and other New Testament characters, (not to say the early so-called Fathers,) to avoid giving them the prefix of "Saint," whether in announcing the lessons in Divine Worship, or in quoting the inspired writers in preaching, as well as on all occasions either public or private. It will assuredly be no loss to these holy men to be deprived of a title never joined to their names in the Bible, or in any of the writings of the Primitive Church, but introduced in corrupt ages by the Church of Rome, and which that apostate system has delighted to bestow, even down to our day, on cruel persecutors and grossly immoral writers! So far from the title "Saint" being peculiar to any one member of the Church, or any one class of its members, we might just as scripturally speak of either Bunyan or Wesley as "Saint" John, as give this style to the writer of the fourth Gospel!

---

## APPENDIX G.

### "THE GREAT ASSIGNED PORTION."

THE first part of 1 Peter v. 3, "neither as lording it over the *great assigned portion* [of God]," is rendered in the Revised Version, "neither as lording it over the charge allotted to you." The Greek is simply τῶν κλήρων, *tōn klērōn*, which is the genitive plural of ὁ κλῆρος, *ho klēros*. This word *klēros* has for its first meaning, "a lot," and for its second, "that which is apportioned by lot," hence, "an assigned portion," and sometimes "an office." This word "lot," used for "an assigned portion," would have great force for Hebrews because the land of Palestine was apportioned amongst their original tribes and families by lot, and it would have scarcely less force for Easterns generally, whose arable lands around the villages are assigned afresh to them each year by the casting of lots, a fact which is not known to the commentators. That *kleros* cannot be "office" here is certain, for no men could "lord it over their offices." It must, therefore, be "*the great assigned portion*," that is, the Church, and whether the Church is to be regarded as "*the great assigned portion*" of God, or of ministers, what student of Scripture can doubt? The Authorised Version speaks of it here as "[God's] heritage," and it would have been well if the Revised Version had followed this Scriptural course, or else had left it indefinite, and simply said, "neither as lording it over *the great assigned portion.*"

I have rendered it "*the great assigned portion*," for only thus are we justified in turning a plural into a singular, as even our Revisers felt that they had to do in this case; "*the great assigned portion*" of the first part of the verse, answering to the one "flock" of the last part, that same "flock" which is called in the preceding verse "the flock of God." This word *kleron* is in fact a "plural of majesty," that is, a plural used to aggrandise a thing that is naturally singular, a Hebrew figure of speech much

more common in the New Testament than is
generally supposed. Thus we read that Christ "sat
down at the right hands of God," that is, at " God's
*great right hand*" (Mark xvi. 19); of "the times
and seasons," that is, " *the great, all-important time
and season*" of the second coming of Christ, when
His people are to be caught up to meet Him in the
air, spoken of just before (1 Thessalonians v. 1; iv.
13—18. See also Acts i. 7, where our Lord uses
the same expression, "times and seasons," of the
one great "time," about which the Apostles had
asked in the last verse); of "the heavenly places "
being purified "with better sacrifices," that is, " with
a better *grand sacrifice*," that of Christ, Who " by
*one offering* perfected " His people (Hebrews ix.
23); of the despisers of Moses' law dying " without
mercies," that is, "without *the least mercy*" (Hebrews
x. 28), &c. &c.

The fact therefore that this word *klērōn* is " a
plural of majesty " meaning " *the great assigned
portion*," "the flock of God " viewed as one, and
belonging to Him, His Own peculiar treasure,
gives considerable force and significance to the
right rendering of the verse: "Neither as lording
it over *the great assigned portion* [of God], but
being *patterns* to the flock," that is, sheep like the
rest,—a part together with them of God's portion,—
who are to be chiefly distinguished from others by
setting a good example. Bishops and priests who
try to exert over the Church the forceful rule so
distinctly forbidden in these words are attempting
to tyrannise over that which does not belong to

them,—that which is not their property or possession, but the property of Another,—"the Church
of God [or "the Lord "] which He has purchased
with His Own blood " (Acts xx. 24).

## APPENDIX H.

### THE EMPHASIS ON "YOUR" AND "FELLOW-WORKERS" IN 2 CORINTHIANS I. 24.

THE order of the words in 2 Corinthians i. 24 is
οὐχ ὅτι κυριεύομεν ὑμῶν τῆς πίστεως, ἀλλὰ συνεργοί ἐσμεν
τῆς χαρᾶς ὑμῶν, *ouchhoti kurieuomen humōn tēs pisteōs,
alla sunergoi esmen tēs charas humōn.* The position
here of ὑμῶν, *humōn,* "*your,*" before, instead of after,
τῆς, *tēs,* or πίστεως, *pisteōs,* "faith," which, as I have
said, makes it emphatic, has, owing to the neglect
of the principles of emphasis, led some commentators, Macknight for instance, to translate the first
part of the verse "not that we lord it over you
[through] faith." But, besides their thus adding
to the text, without any warrant, the preposition
"through," they actually justify this rendering by
saying that the Apostles *had* lordship over their
converts' faith ! The emphasis on "*fellow-
workers*" appears by this word in Greek, συνεργοί,
*sunergoi,* being placed before, instead of after, the
verb ἐσμεν, *esmen,* "we are."

# APPENDIX I.

THAT this verse, 2 Corinthians i. 24, really requires
the rendering that I have given, seems plain from
the use of the word "*fellow-workers.*" If Paul
merely meant that Apostles and ministers laboured
to promote the joy of the laity, he would simply
have said, we are "workers of your joy," not as he
does, "*fellow-workers ;*" or else, on the other hand,
in the former member of the verse, he would have
said "have lordship-*together* over your faith,"
whereas he only says "have lordship." In the
way I have translated it, the verse becomes powerful and perfectly consistent, and exhibits a bold
and striking contrast. So far was the Apostle
from claiming dominion over the faith of his
brethren in Christ, that, on the contrary, he pre-
ferred to represent himself as one of their "*joyful
fellow-workers,*" laying a marked emphasis, as he
does, on each of these two words.

I say on *each* of the words, for the reader should
observe that this lengthened form of the attribute
—namely, the use of a noun preceded by the sign
of the genitive case, instead of a simple adjective,
which is such a peculiar and picturesque idiom of
Hebrew and all its cognate tongues,—and hence
has crept so constantly into the New Testament,
owing to its inspired writers being Hebrews,—is
distinctly an *emphatic form,·* a point which I be-

lieve has escaped the notice of most of the grammarians. Alford and others, it is true, have carefully noted this form, and have called attention to the fact that the person or thing in this case is said to belong to the virtue, vice, or other abstract quality, placed in the genitive. But they have failed to note that this figure of speech is simply a forcible Hebrew, Eastern way of naming an attribute.

The Greek grammarians speak of this figure as if it were limited to abstract qualities only, such as virtues, vices, &c., whereas, in Hebrew, concrete nouns are used in this way equally with abstract ones. Thus, "from the hands of a man of his brother" is "from the hands of his *brother* man" (Genesis ix. 5); "a people of a prince that shall come" is "a *princely* people that shall come" (Daniel ix. 26), &c. This is just the same in the Biblical Greek of the New Testament, where "the kingdom of heaven" is "the *heavenly* kingdom" (Matthew iii. 2); "the Son of Man is "the *Human* Son or Person" (Matthew xvi. 27); "the Gehenna of fire" is "the *fiery* Gehenna" (Matthew v. 22), the figure of hell. In this way, "lusts of dishonour" (Romans i. 26) is a figure of speech, by which "lusts" are represented as belonging to "dishonour" as its own peculiar possession. But the true force of this figure put into literal English is "*dishonourable* lusts." The Apostle James is using a stronger expression with reference to the attribute of meekness in the words "meekness of wisdom" (James iii. 13) than if he

had simply joined the adjective " wise " to the noun
"meekness," though the expression "*wise* meekness " is the only clear idiomatic way of rendering
it in our language. This construction is called
*hendiadys*, from the Greek words *hen dia duoin* (one
by means of two), because one idea is conveyed
by two words. Though very characteristic of the
New Testament, it is not peculiar to Biblical
Greek, for it is frequently found in good classical
writers.

The Revised Version of the New Testament
has rendered this figure of *hendiadys*, in most of
the instances where it is used, with a close adher-
ence to the Greek form, which, though often pro-
ducing ungrammatical English, at all events enables
the unlearned reader to trace its occurrence.
" Fellow-workers of your joy," is, therefore, a
strong emphatic way of expressing " joyful "—
"your *joyful* fellow-workers." I have already
shown that the word "*fellow-workers*" is also
emphatic from its place in the sentence. Thus,
by the position of both the words "fellow-workers"
and "joy," emphasis has, with great skill, been laid
upon each !

May, 1885, Fcap. 8vo, bound, **1s. 6d.**; limp cloth, **1s.**

# KISSING : ITS CURIOUS BIBLE MENTIONS.

### By JAMES NEIL, M.A.,

*Formerly Incumbent of Christ Church, Jerusalem.*

Publishers: SIMPKIN, MARSHALL, & Co., 4, Stationers' Hall Court, London.

---

## OTHER WORKS BY THE SAME AUTHOR.

Eighth Edition, 1883, Crown 8vo, handsomely bound, **3s.**

# PALESTINE RE-PEOPLED ; OR, SCATTERED ISRAEL'S GATHERING, A SIGN OF THE TIMES. With a new Preface treating of recent events. This work shows that the Jews are now returning to Palestine, what the Scriptures foretell will follow, and what they say of Russia.

" Some readers would pore over it with a delight almost amounting to rapture."—*Literary World.*

" Should by all means be read by those who take any interest in Scripture prophecy. . . . He writes with a full grasp of his subject, and in an admirable spirit."—*Edinburgh Daily Review.*

" The topic is replete with attraction and excitement."—*Study.*

" Of great value and intense interest."—*Israel's Watchman.*

" Peculiarly interesting."—*Christian.*

N.B.—The first copies of this work that reached St. Petersburg were seized by the censors of the Russian press, and returned to the publishers with an intimation that no others would be allowed to enter the dominions of the Czar!

Published by J. NISBET & Co., 21, Berners Street, London.

---

Fifth Edition, 1882, Extra Crown 8vo, handsomely bound, **2s. 6d.**

# RAYS FROM THE REALMS OF NATURE ; OR, PARABLES OF PLANT-LIFE. With Coloured Frontispiece and 50 Engravings.

" Beautifully got up, profusely illustrated by charming engravings."—*School Guardian.*

"A very richly illustrated work, and one of rare originality."—*English Churchman.*

"Lessons drawn from nature, and so arranged as to symbolise almost all the passions and principles of human life."—*Edinburgh Daily Review.*

"Will take a good place no doubt amongst the best books of its class. Mr. Neil shows both poetic taste and profound reverence for the written word."—*Clergyman's Magazine.*

"This is a book after our own heart . . . will secure a numerous host of readers."—*Sword and Trowel.*

"A most important, as well as an intensely interesting, book. A treat seldom met with."—*Christian Progress.*

Published by CASSELL & Co., 4A, Belle Sauvage Yard, London.

---

Second Edition, 1883, Crown 8vo, cloth gilt, 6s.

## PALESTINE EXPLORED, WITH A VIEW TO ITS PRESENT NATURAL FEATURES, AND TO THE PREVAILING MANNERS, CUSTOMS, RITES, AND COLLOQUIAL EXPRESSIONS OF ITS PEOPLE, WHICH THROW LIGHT ON THE FIGURATIVE LANGUAGE OF THE BIBLE. Frontispiece and six full-page original Drawings. This work of 319 pages gives a popular account of discoveries made by the author in Palestine, which throw new light on the Bible.

"Extremely interesting, and valuable as illustrations of the Bible."—*Palestine Exploration Fund Quarterly Statement.*

"A work of rich Biblical knowledge, and of a degree of originality which we should hardly have thought possible at the present day."—*Clergyman's Magazine.*

"Full of really valuable illustrations and explanations of Biblical facts and phrases."—*Guardian.*

"Many figures of which we have never realised the force now seem to glow with light."—*Word and Work.*

"A book abounding with original and striking illustrations of Scripture."—Dr. Geikie's *Hours with the Bible*, vol. iv., p. 350.

Published by J. NISBET & Co., 21, Berners Street, London.

www.ingramcontent.com/pod-product-compliance
Lightning Source LLC
Chambersburg PA
CBHW020027030726
47499CB00007B/2307